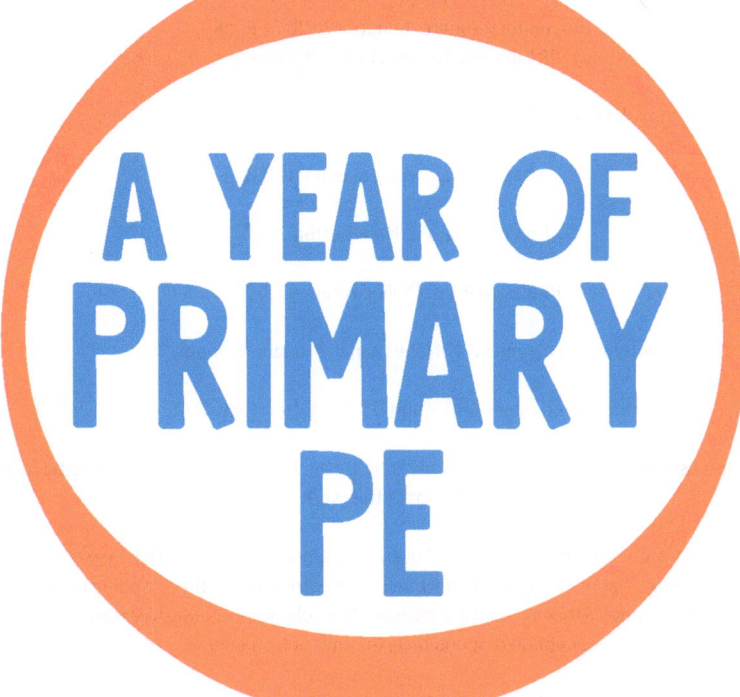

A YEAR OF PRIMARY PE

110 games to support
whole-child development
from September to July

MARK CARTER

BLOOMSBURY EDUCATION

LONDON   OXFORD   NEW YORK   NEW DELHI   SYDNEY

BLOOMSBURY EDUCATION
Bloomsbury Publishing Plc
50 Bedford Square, London, WC1B 3DP, UK
29 Earlsfort Terrace, Dublin 2, Ireland

A catalogue record for this book is available from the British Library

ISBN: PB: 978-1-4729-9223-9; ePDF: 978-1-4729-9222-2

2 4 6 8 10 9 7 5 3 1 (paperback)

Text design by Jeni Child

Printed and bound in India by Replika Press Pvt. Ltd

To find out more about our authors and books visit www.bloomsbury.com and sign up for our newsletters

Contents

Key: ☒ = These games can be played by a class of 30 children in a small space.

🟨 = These games require no equipment or can be easily adapted to be played with no equipment.

🟥 KS2 = These games are more complex and are therefore suitable for Key Stage 2 classes only.

Children waiting in lines to read a book. We would never actually teach reading like this. So why does PE so often look like this?

Acknowledgements

Thanks to Team MJMH – for support, love and play.

With thanks to:

- Isla Findlay (and Hanover Primary School, Islington)
- Karl Beckford (and Canonbury Primary School, Islington)
- Nahdeannah Francis-Pennant (and Rotherfield Primary School, Islington)
- my book advisory group of Creag Lawrence, Karl Beckford, Lawrence Lok, Laura McBain, Sharon Muxworthy and Chris Welburn
- the Future Zone PE Network, Islington
- the Arsenal in the Community Primary Education team
- the FA PE Unit delivery team, 2017–2020
- Ministry of Football children, families and coaches, 2007–2020
- teachers, tutors and academics who have reviewed chapters and offered ideas and feedback.

Introduction

I first taught in Papua New Guinea, working with classes of up to 55 children, with no textbooks and no internet. My only teaching tool was a piece of chalk. It was difficult and I struggled, and I really wished I had a book that told me what and how to teach. I then became Director of Youth Coaching at the largest sports club in New Zealand, supporting professional and volunteer coaches to deliver age-appropriate football programmes that addressed the different and varied needs of the children they worked with. This involved adapting the overuse of large-sided, adult-focused drills and games they had learned about during courses, in booklets or on the internet.

Since returning to London in 2007, I have set up and directed the Ministry of Football skill development programme, led the PE Network for Future Zone, Islington, and spent three years at the Football Association's 'PE Unit', working with teachers and trainee teachers to help improve their confidence and competence to teach PE. All these experiences have allowed me to explore my passion for play, understand the difficulties that teachers and coaches have when working with primary-aged children, and appreciate the need for guidance when many practitioners have had very little access to training, support or resources.

This book is a result of my accumulated experience teaching games to children aged five to 11. I hope you find it useful.

About the book

The intention of this book is to help teachers deliver units of games lessons that engage and include every child in their class and teach children a broad range of holistic skills.

The book challenges traditional models of primary school PE. It sees the subject as an integral and powerful part of the school curriculum and an opportunity for holistic child development. Future society, communities and families need children to grow up into adults who are responsible, courageous, fair and kind. As teachers, we have a duty to raise children who make a positive difference to the world. School is a place where children can learn to be kinder and braver, and PE can play a vital and essential part in this process.

To achieve this, schools can link their intentions for PE to ambitious whole-school development targets. This book provides a framework for the development of holistic skills through PE by focusing on essential skills like 'working together' and 'being part of a team'. By developing these skills, we help children grow into employable, responsible and successful citizens.

The book follows the academic year, from September to July. Rather than focusing on specific sports, each month has a learning theme focused on holistic skills development and linked to the National Curriculum. The 11 monthly learning themes are carefully ordered and can be broadly grouped into three sections:

● September to December: We start the year with a focus on social skills and relationship building, working with the children to build a positive and respectful culture across the school. Children will learn how to work together, include everyone, challenge themselves and solve problems. By teaching these skills early in the year, we build the capacity of children to collaborate and take responsibility for deeper learning in PE after Christmas.

- January to April: In the spring term, we practise and develop the children's movement skills and ability to attack and defend in games. January and February focus on the four movement skills mentioned in the National Curriculum: throwing, catching, running and jumping. In March and April, we use a variety of age-appropriate games to develop children's understanding and decision-making in invasion, net and wall, striking and fielding, and target games.

- May to July: We complete the year with deeper themes exploring competition, responsibility and the meaning of movement. Themes provide for the children's broader development, enabling them to develop and discover their sports interests and their own unique relationship with movement. During the last two months of the year, we consider the role of ethics and equality in competition.

Developing movement skills in PE

'Fundamental movement skills' is a broad term used for a variety of movements, four of which are mentioned in the PE National Curriculum for Key Stage 1 (KS1) and Key Stage 2 (KS2): throwing, catching, running and jumping. The term might also include other locomotive actions like skipping, rolling or sliding; stability skills like twisting, landing or turning; and object control skills like bowling, dribbling or striking.

Most primary school classroom teachers are provided with little or no training in how to teach movement skills. It is not the intention of this book to develop teachers who are experts in teaching movement techniques. There are two chapters, January and February, which focus specifically on the development of movement skills and some teaching guidance is provided in these chapters. For the rest of the year, the intention is that children will learn to move by moving, rather than being taught to move by their teacher.

The games in this book have been selected and designed to maximise the amount of time that children spend in movement. Where possible, all the children are involved all the time – there is little or no queuing or waiting time – and movements are given purpose by being linked to the game being played. The role of the teacher is to carefully consider how to set up and deliver games to maximise movement opportunities and to encourage exploration of new movements or combinations of movements.

Holistic development and the PE National Curriculum

The development of movement skills is only one part of a much wider remit for physical education. To regard the aims of the subject as solely physical is inaccurate and unambitious. The subject has far more potential and power than that.

Below, sections of the KS1 and KS2 PE National Curriculum in England are restructured to show how they provide for holistic development across four skill areas. This information is provided to show which parts of the PE National Curriculum are covered by this book and to encourage teachers to focus their PE lessons on holistic skills in the knowledge that such an approach is aligned with the intended outcomes for the subject.

Movement skills

Become physically confident in a way that supports fitness; lead active lives; be physically active for sustained periods of time.

- KS1: Develop fundamental movement skills; master basic movements including throwing, catching, running and jumping; develop agility, balance and coordination.

- KS2: Use running, jumping, throwing and catching in isolation and in combination; make actions and sequences of movements; develop flexibility, strength, technique, control and balance.

Sport skills

Engage in competitive sports and activities.

- KS1: Participate in team games; develop simple tactics for attacking and defending.

- KS2: Develop a broader range of skills; play competitive games, modified where appropriate; apply basic principles of attacking and defending.

Thinking skills

- KS1: Apply learning in increasingly challenging situations; become increasingly confident; compete with self and others; apply skills in a range of activities.

- KS2: Apply a broader range of skills, learning how to use them and link them; develop an understanding of how to improve; learn how to evaluate and recognise own success; compare their performances with previous ones and demonstrate improvement to achieve their personal best.

People skills

Build character and help to embed values such as fairness and respect.

- KS1: Engage in cooperative activities.

- KS2: Enjoy communicating, collaborating and competing with others.

How to teach PE: learning through games

This is a book of games and about learning through games. However, the games in this book don't look like the adult versions of familiar sports. Instead, they are miniaturised versions, deliberately modified to reduce player numbers, limit space or change rules in order for every child to experience many repetitions of similar situations. It is through these repeated episodes of problem-solving, decision-making or movement solutions that learning can happen – especially when time is also spent reflecting and reviewing these decisions and solutions.

A game is any activity that has (i) rules and (ii) a quantifiable outcome (Salen and Zimmerman, 2004). A quantifiable outcome could include a way of scoring, progressing, completing or winning. By this definition, every activity in this book is a game. In addition, every game in this book engages the children cognitively through an element of decision-making or a problem to solve. The games in this book include opportunities to practise techniques and movements but also help children explore and practise why, where and

when to use these techniques and movements in realistic game situations. At a deeper level, a game is a microcosm of society – with the same reliance on relationships, rules and responsibility. By using games in PE, we can explore being fair, being kind and being inclusive – and relate these values to the children's lives inside and outside of school.

I have tested every one of the 110 games in this book in a primary school setting. They have all worked well, although some required more adaptation than others (especially for younger classes). There are lots of individual, pair and small-group activities, which all children play at the same time. Where the children are in teams, the number of players is limited to increase participation levels and allow several games to take place in a small space at the same time. I have tried to limit games where children perform an action in front of all their classmates and there is only one activity in the whole book that involves a queue.

Reference
- Salen, K. and Zimmerman, E. (2004), *Rules of Play*. Cambridge, MA: MIT Press.

Play versus instruction

When teaching games, it can be difficult to find the right balance between play and instruction. Children are usually quite capable of making up their own games and learning through their own game play. However, as teachers responsible for delivering the curriculum, we must plan and direct the children's learning towards specific outcomes. The subject cannot therefore be play in its truest sense. When pondering the right balance of instruction and liberty, it may be helpful for teachers to consider providing the children with 'freedom within a framework' – the 'framework' being the teacher's non-negotiable conditions that ensure specific learning is explored, and the 'freedom' being the children's choice and responsibility to invent and explore within that framework.

The exact amount of freedom you offer will depend on your confidence and the maturity and skill of the children to use the freedom sensibly. It should be noted that even very young children can be given elements of choice and responsibility (for example, which size ball to use) and expected to solve a variety of problems (for example, finding their own partner to work with, taking care of their own equipment and setting up their own areas).

Even young children should be given responsibility, ownership and choice.

Summative assessment in PE

Monitoring pupil progress through summative assessment is critical in every subject across the primary curriculum. Just because children are learning through games, it does not mean that assessment in PE is any less vital, although assessment methods are likely to differ from classroom subjects such as English and mathematics.

Every primary school context is unique, every primary school class is different from others, and every child within each class is an individual. Therefore, we might question the relevance of

skill progression documents that describe exactly what each child should achieve by the end of each school year. Instead, it might be wise for teachers to develop their own descriptions of skill development intentions based on their knowledge of their school, class and children.

A list of key skills is provided at the beginning of each chapter. This includes eight skill areas that are the focus of the games and assessment for learning questions in that chapter. It is intended that teachers use their knowledge of their own context to determine appropriate success criteria for each theme. These success criteria (or the theme as a whole) can then be used to assess progress, provide feedback to parents and plan future teaching.

When assessing children's attainment in PE, consider your own context (e.g. school values and the purpose of your PE curriculum), assess across multiple domains (social skills are just as important as physical development) and consider including child voice in your assessment. Here are three examples of summative assessment methods that you may want to consider and adapt.

Using school values and the purpose of PE

The first table on page xi assesses children against four typical primary school values (e.g. working hard) using a simple grading system:

- **K**now: The children can explain the key points verbally.

- **U**nderstand: The children can demonstrate the key points.

- **A**pply: The children can put the key points into practice in a variety of contexts.

This kind of data can help measure a child's progress from one year to the next and can help a new class teacher by providing useful information on each child.

The final three columns assess progress in 'promoting movement and encouraging physical activity' (a potential purpose of PE), using data from after-school clubs, observations of playtimes and a parent–child questionnaire on physical activity outside of school. Taken together these three metrics may provide an overview of the level of physical activity each child engages in. This data could provide a measurable baseline from which to assess the impact of PE as a vehicle for inspiring children to engage in voluntary movement. These columns are scored as follows:

- After-school sport clubs this year so far: This is the number of clubs each child has attended so far this academic year.

- Movement at play and lunchtimes: This metric is based on observations from playground supervisors and expresses the extent to which each child engages in movement at play and lunchtimes (H = high, M = medium, L = low).

- Physical activity outside school: This metric is based on a parent–child questionnaire which asks how much weekly physical activity each child takes part in outside of school (H = high, M = medium, L = low).

Using learning themes

The table below includes the first eight learning themes from this book. For each child, the teacher has highlighted two areas they are most able in and two they are least able in. In addition, each child has reported their own favourite area and their level of enjoyment of PE. This assessment allows teachers to determine growth areas for specific children, identify children who may be less engaged with the subject, and evaluate the overall success of engagement and learning across the different themes.

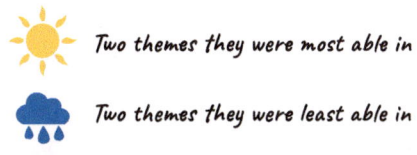

Two themes they were most able in

Two themes they were least able in

Child's favourite theme so far

	School values				Purpose of PE: promoting movement and encouraging physical activity		
Know (can say) **U**nderstand (can demonstrate) **A**pply (can use in a variety of contexts)	Working hard	Respecting each other	Supporting each other to succeed	Being kind	After-school sport clubs this year so far	Movement at play and lunchtimes	Physical activity outside school
Dino	A	U	U	U	4	H	M
Maya	A	A	A	U	2	M	M
Hannah	K	U	U	U	1	L	M
Zach	U	K	K	U	0	L	L
Amy	A	A	K	A	0	L	L
Kyri	U	A	A	U	3	M	M
Amira	A	U	K	U	1	M	H
Khadija	U	U	K	U	0	H	M
Max	A	U	A	A	2	L	M
Zoe	K	A	K	U	2	H	H

	How much do you enjoy PE?	Working together	Thinking of others	Challenging yourself	Problem-solving	Throwing and catching skills	Running and jumping skills	Defending skills	Attacking skills
Dino	😕	☀	☀	☁		☁	■		
Maya	🙂			☁	☁		☀		■
Hannah	🙂		☀		■			☁	☁
Zach	🙂			☁		☀		☁	■
Amy	🙂		☀		☁	☁			■
Kyri	😕	☁	■	☀		☁	☀		
Amira	🙂			■	☀	☁	☁		
Khadija	🙂	☁	■	☀		☀	☁		
Max	🙂		☀	☁		☀		☁	■
Zoe	🙂	☀		■	☁	☁	☀		

Using four skill areas: movement, sport, thinking and people

On page viii, the PE National Curriculum for KS1 and KS2 is broken down into four skill areas. This framework could provide a useful basis for identifying focus areas for development and for assessing the progress of children. In this example, a simple numerical scoring system is used. Again, progress can be tracked throughout primary school and key focus areas identified for the class or individuals within it.

4 = advanced 3 = above average 2 = average 1 = development needed	Movement skills	Sport skills	Thinking skills	People skills
Dino	2	1	3	4
Maya	4	4	2	3
Hannah	3	3	3	4
Zach	2	2	3	2
Amy	2	3	3	4
Kyri	3	4	2	1
Amira	2	2	1	4
Khadija	2	4	2	2
Max	3	4	4	1
Zoe	2	2	1	4

PE for every child

The way we teach PE matters. PE typically works best for those children who are most like the teacher, and we would do well to consider how we engage and include those who are least like us.

Traditionally, PE has placed a high value on competitiveness, fitness and physical dominance. However, in order to include everyone and to be relevant for every child in a primary school, PE teaching (and teachers) must widen the definitions of success to include friendship, respect and working well with others. Through PE, we can teach children to understand and appreciate diversity and promote respectful and inclusive behaviours.

We need to find ways of including children in the design of PE programmes and to find ways to listen to their views. We especially need to consider: 'Whose voices are not being heard?' PE curricula should be culturally relevant. Democratic PE means the teacher gives up some of their own power, and hands it over to the students. We should work hard to identify and remove the barriers that prevent some children from being involved.

'The A–Z of social justice in physical education' (by Dr Shrehan Lynch et al., 2020) is a must-read for primary teachers and leaders. Here is a summary of their top tips for a socially just PE programme:

1 Take time to **get to know your children** and how they identify. Each one of them is different. Success will depend on getting to know them as individuals.

2 Provide time early in the year for the children to **create their own class behaviour rules and expectations**. Revisit these rules and expectations throughout the year.

3 Encourage and allow children to **create and develop their own PE programme**. Teach the value of a democratic approach where children share ownership and evaluation of their lessons and learning.

4 **Take on the role of a facilitator** rather than a commander. Even with young children, aim to help them lead aspects of their own learning and take responsibility for their environment and experiences.

Wheelchair users

There are several games in this book which can be played by children who use a wheelchair. Obviously, the exact adaptations needed will depend on the specific, individual needs of each child, but games like Sitting Volleyball (page 52), Blindfold Boccia (page 192), Battleships (page 109) and Beanbag Golf (page 34) could be ideal options for teachers with wheelchair users in their class. There may be adapted roles for wheelchair users in many other games too. For example, wheelchair users could join throwing games like Magic Three (page 214), Moving Target (page 198) and Shoot for the Stars (page 68). Again, the adaptation needed will depend on the specific needs of the child.

Including girls in PE

Teachers need to consider how to include and engage every girl and every boy in their PE lessons. Recent action research on girls' physical activity levels (from the Youth Sport Trust and Loughborough University) recommends: consulting with less active girls; engaging parents; training school staff; promoting positive role models; and providing opportunities for girls to be leaders. The full report and further information are available at this link: www.youthsporttrust.org/news-insight/research-papers/engaging-girls.

Colour blindness

Colour blindness affects one in 12 boys (eight per cent) and one in 200 girls. There are approximately three million colour-blind people in the UK, and 450,000 are school children – that's one in every classroom! When using coloured bibs for team games, try to have one colour as white or yellow and the other as red, blue or black.

For more advice on delivering colour-blind-friendly PE and sport, visit: www.colourblindawareness.org/colour-blindness-and-sport/coaching-kit-and-equipment.

More information

- Lynch, S., Sutherland, S. and Walton-Fisette, J. (2020), 'The A-Z of social justice in physical education: Part 1', *Journal of PE, Recreation and Dance*, 91, (4), 8–13.
- PhysEquity is a social change movement with a vision of equitable PE. Resources, publications, blogs and podcasts can be found at: https://physequity.wordpress.com.

How to use this book

The book is divided into 11 monthly chapters, each with a learning theme. These learning themes build on each other throughout the year to develop children's skills and combine to cover most of the PE National Curriculum for KS1 and KS2. However, in some school contexts it may be appropriate to re-order the chapters or spend longer on some than others. Individual schools and teachers will need to consider their children and context and select the most useful themes to focus on.

It is important to point out that this book does not cover the entire PE National Curriculum for KS1 and KS2. The book does not cover elements on dance, swimming or outdoor adventurous activities. It is suggested that this book could be used to plan and deliver one PE lesson a week, while a second weekly lesson is used for remaining elements of the National Curriculum.

Quick starter games and main games

Each chapter contains five quick starter games and five main games. This allows a deep exploration of each month's theme across a broad and varied range of different sports, experiences and contexts.

● Quick starter games: These are games that don't take long to set up. They are perfect for when you arrive in the hall or playground and you want to get the children moving soon. You could use a quick starter game to keep the children engaged and learning while you set up a main game. You could also use a quick starter to introduce learning or vocabulary or recap previous learning.

● Main games: These are games that may take a little longer to set up or involve more explanation. They are typically games that have more progressions and adaptations. Some might be perfect to explore over more than one lesson.

You don't have to do all the games in the book, and you don't have to do them in the order they appear.

The vast majority of the games can be adapted to suit all primary age groups. However, some games will suit younger classes better than others, and there is one game each month labelled as 'KS2 only' because I really don't think it would work with seven-year-olds no matter how you adapted it.

When adapting a pairs activity for a class with an odd number of children, consider having one group of three. You could play two against one, for example. Older children may be able to work out a good way of including the extra player. For small-sided games, children should get used to games of unequal numbers. It is fine to play four versus three or five versus four; in fact it can be a really useful way of evening up matches and offering appropriate levels of challenge and support (see the STEP framework on page 61).

Adaptations

In my experience, children in the same year group can be hugely different from each other. In two-form-entry schools, it is common for one Year 3 class to be very different from the other Year 3 class. I have not therefore prescribed games to specific year groups. Rather I have suggested adaptations to games, which will help teachers consider how they could amend the game to make it fit for their class.

Assessment for learning

Each game is accompanied by suggestions for assessment for learning (AfL) questions. These discussions are equally as important as the games themselves. Children's learning is enhanced through social interaction and dialogue brokered through their physical involvement in the game.

Discussions on game understanding should be preceded and followed by opportunities to play the game. The questions are intended to be asked after the children have explored the game (not before). The exploration of the game provides the basis for the dialogue that follows. In most cases - especially if the questions are about game understanding or tactics – the children should get a further chance to explore the game after the dialogue. The discussion may have helped spark new ideas or share understanding, and children then need the opportunity to experience the game with this new knowledge and motivation.

> Choose the games, adaptations and assessment for learning questions that you think will work for your class.

Classroom debates

Teachers should aim to find classroom time for longer discussions on the learning themes. To aid these discussions, each theme contains some deeper questions and recommended classroom debates. When using these, teachers will need to facilitate conversations and reflections, helping children grow their ability to listen, to comprehend and to disagree with each other, and to build their capacity to determine right and wrong together.

Cross-curricular links

The games in the book provide regular opportunities to link learning in PE with learning in other subject areas. Examples of these are included in each chapter.

Top tips

Many games contain a 'top tip', typically something which may make the game work better or a way of teaching or delivering the game which may be more suitable in some settings.

'How to' sections

In addition to the games, there are a selection of 'How to' pages at the beginning of each chapter, related to the learning theme or the time of year. These are intended to offer advice and 'top tips' for teachers to help them transfer their teaching and learning skills from the classroom to the PE hall or playground.

For teachers who are considering using a models-based approach to PE, a variety of models

are described in further 'How to' pages and accompanied by one game that demonstrates the model in action. Further reading is suggested on each page.

Putting it all together: possible ways to structure a games lesson

There are a variety of different ways in which you can piece together the activities in this book to structure an effective games lesson. I've offered five possible options below. The most important thing to remember is to keep your lesson simple. One or two games per lesson, with progressions and time for discussion, is realistic.

> ### Option 1
> A selection of quick starters in a carousel (see page 97)

> ### Option 2
> A quick starter then a main game

> ### Option 3
> A main game (explored over more than one lesson)

> ### Option 4
> Main → Quick starter → Main
> (using the whole-part-whole structure – see page 126)

> ### Option 5
> Different groups within the class do different games (e.g. according to preference)

The photography

For this book, I have worked with photographer Philipp Ammon to capture KS1 and KS2 PE at three schools in Islington, London. Where possible, we have selected photographs that help show how each game is set up or played. We know that teachers are often short of time, and that a good picture might show how the game works much more efficiently than rows of text.

As well as showing the games in action, the photography celebrates primary PE in an inner-city setting. Philipp worked as a 'fly on the wall' while I taught the lessons, and the results are evidence of what PE is like in these schools. The photographs are meant to be realistic and attainable, not perfect. PE isn't always neat and tidy; children don't always remember their PE kit and not every child is focused or on-task all the time. I hope the pictures provide you with reassurance that it's OK for PE to look a bit messy.

Photo by Nahdeannah
Francis-Pennant.

Companion website

Use the QR code or visit pekitchen.org to access the website which supports this book and provides free content including lesson planners and videos of some of the games in action.

Generic pitch set-ups

The set-up we use in games is important. We need to keep things simple, but we also want to arrange things so children get to play and move in lessons as much as possible. Several games in this book use similar set-ups and these are shown in the following diagrams.

Normal pitch

Used in:
- Press or Drop? (page 146)
- Rollercoaster (page 108)
- Netball Legends 2 (page 92)

Pitch with a goal or targets

End zones

Used in:
- Team Ball (page 55)
- Invisiball (page 162)
- Ultimate (page 32)

End zones   Three small courts for a class of 30

Half court

Used in:
- Spiderman (page 45)
- Kabaddi (page 221)
- Capture the Flag (page 161)
- Battleships (page 109)

Half court   Three small courts for a class of 30

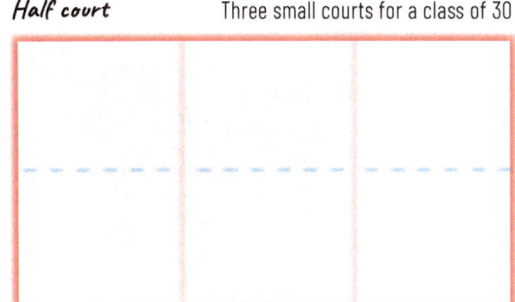

Striking and fielding

Used in:
- Noodle Rounders (page 50)
- Field of Dreams (page 144)
- Super Striker (page 73)
- The Empire Strikes Back (page 166)
- Diamond Strike (page 204)

Small-sided striking and fielding

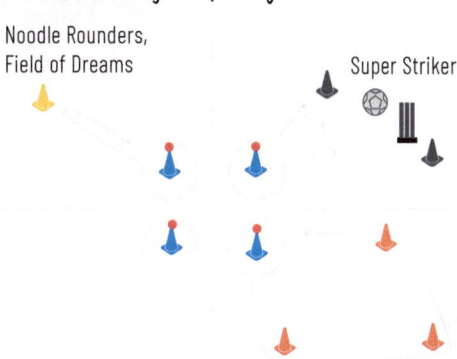

Noodle Rounders, Field of Dreams

Super Striker

The Empire Strikes Back, Diamond Strike

September

Working together

National Curriculum links

KS1:

'Pupils should be able to engage in competitive and cooperative physical activities, in a range of increasingly challenging situations.'

KS2:

'Pupils should enjoy communicating, collaborating and competing with each other.'

An introduction to working together

September is all about setting expectations and starting to teach the social skills needed to work together and play fairly. Don't worry too much about teaching sport or movement techniques, rather focus on getting to know your class and helping them learn to get on with each other. It is essential that children understand the basic expectations of sharing and taking turns in PE. The work you do this month will lay a vital foundation for the rest of the year.

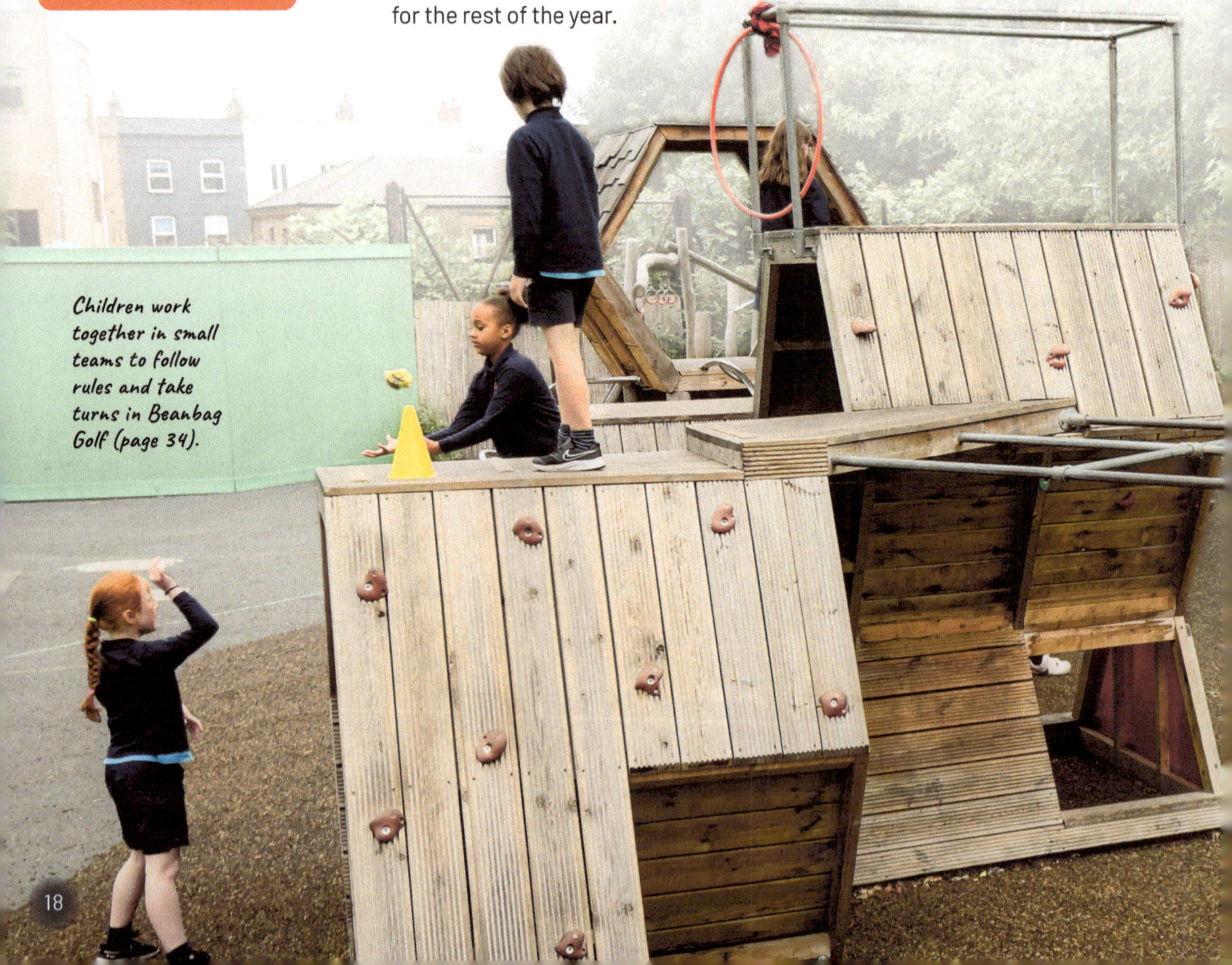

Children work together in small teams to follow rules and take turns in Beanbag Golf (page 34).

Cooperation can be difficult for many children, especially during competition, which is a major part of the National Curriculum at KS1 and KS2. Many children struggle to follow rules, play fairly, win with grace or accept defeat. The assessment for learning questions in Beanbag Golf (page 34), Duels (page 28) and Ultimate (page 32) will help to start conversations which explore how we work together when we are competing. Top tips this month (page 21) look at how to prevent and manage arguments and disputes in PE and help children resolve these situations on their own.

On page 33, we focus on cooperative learning. This is an approach to grouping children and assigning tasks which encourages children to work together and to take responsibility for their own learning. This is a useful approach to adopt, especially for the first part of the school year, as it can help to explore and embed key social and collaborative skills. Many children will not be used to helping, supporting and encouraging each other, and it may take several weeks of consistent work to progress from group work to teamwork. (This process is explored further in the June chapter about being part of a team.)

Key skills

- Sharing equipment and space with others
- Finding a partner and working with a range of different partners
- Taking turns, listening to each other and sharing ideas
- Playing fairly, keeping score and following rules
- Playing larger group games and devising tactics together
- Leading others and being led by others
- Competing against each other, to win and lose
- Resolving disputes

How to start a game efficiently

Time is precious in PE lessons! You need to find ways of showing, setting up and starting games which are time efficient. You can help manage the children's behaviour by limiting the amount of time they spend sitting and listening to your instructions.

1 Ensure equipment is accessible

If you are using footballs, for example, make sure they aren't tied up in a bag. If each child will need to get two cones, don't have them all in one big pile; instead spread them out into several smaller piles. You want to allow children to find their own equipment sensibly and efficiently.

2 Get the children to gather round

Arrange the children so they can all see and hear your demonstration. A semi-circle works well, or a huddle can work too. Sitting the children down usually works better than having them standing up. Avoid a long line of children as those on either end can't hear or see and are harder to manage and engage.

3 Show or present the game

Demonstrate the game or show it on a whiteboard. This should be a quick demo, without lots of technical information. Start with the space or area and any boundaries. Then show the basic task, along with any rules that are non-negotiable. Teaching and questioning should be left until later, once you have observed what the children can and can't do.

4 Let them set it up themselves

Simply: 'Find a partner, get your equipment and off you go!' Allow the children to take responsibility for their own setting-up. The children will get better at this if given enough opportunities. You may need to offer them some occasional feedback on how you think they are doing at this.

5 Help individuals who are struggling

Your role may now be to help those who are struggling with the rules, space or instructions, or who cannot find a partner or group. If the same children continually struggle with this part of the lesson, support them by teaching them how they could improve. For example, to find a partner, they need to look around and make eye contact with someone who also seems to be looking for a partner.

> **Top TIP**
> Where possible, demonstrate the game first, before children are in pairs, groups or teams.

Resolving disputes

You may sometimes find that disputes arise between children in PE. Here are some top tips to help you manage these disputes and support children in resolving them independently.

Five top tips to manage disputes among children in PE

1 Play as small groups

It can be difficult for young children to resolve disputes when they are in large teams or groups. An argument happening in a seven-a-side netball game may stop half the class from playing and learning. We can make it easier for children by reducing team or group size or game format. This reduces the skill level needed to resolve the conflict and makes it more likely that they will solve issues themselves without your input.

2 Use games

Make the game so good that the children don't want to waste their game time with arguments. Make it clear to the children: you can either carry on arguing or you can sort it out and get on with the game.

3 Isolate

Remove the children who are arguing from the main group. Bring the children who are arguing over to you and ask the rest of the group or class to continue their activity. This means that you and the children involved can deal with the situation without pressure from spectators.

4 Separate

If specific children cannot seem to cooperate in the same game or group, then you may need to separate them and have them play in different games or groups. This should only be a temporary solution though, so make a note and find a time when you can discuss the situation with them and help them progress towards more collaborative behaviours.

5 Teach

If children haven't learnt to cooperate with each other, then maybe cooperation hasn't been taught well enough yet. Create some classroom time to discuss cooperation in PE. The strategies below should help you consider what to teach.

Four ways for children to work together to resolve their own disputes in PE

1 Remind

Remind each other of the rules. This should be the first method children are taught. It may be that someone has forgotten or not understood the rules. A friendly reminder should be the first step.

2 Replay

Children in disagreement could choose to replay or restart the game from a point before the disagreement began. So, if they are arguing over who caught a frisbee in Ultimate (page 32), then take the game back to the person who made the throw and replay it. To prevent this from happening too often, you could allow each team to have three chances for a replay per game.

3 Referee

You should not get involved in refereeing PE games. You are a teacher, not a referee. But you could choose one of the children to referee the game; this brings opportunities for some important teaching and learning about respecting the referee's decision.

4 Rock-paper-scissors

This simple solution is quick and fun. The two players arguing face off in one round of rock-paper-scissors to end the argument and continue the game.

Bubble burst

A fun popping game in a bubbly atmosphere.

How to facilitate the game

1 Set expectations. Explain to the class that they are going to be working together with bubbles. Tell them the rules: they must move and play gently and they are not allowed to pop the bubbles (to begin with). Their first challenge will be to see if they can catch a bubble in their hands.

2 Play. Spread the children out and blow lots of bubbles into the air. The more adults you have to blow bubbles, the better this will work.

Adaptations

This activity works best for younger children, but there are various ways to add different tasks and challenges for more able or older children too.

↑ Can you balance on one leg and catch a bubble in your hand?

↑ Can you hold a hula hoop and move the hoop around a bubble without popping it? (Two children could hold a hoop together to add a 'working together' challenge.)

↑ Can you work as a team to make sure none of the bubbles reach the floor (by popping them, or by blowing air at the bubbles from underneath)?

Assessment for learning

This can be a challenging activity for young children. They will be looking at the bubbles while they are moving, but they also need to look out for each other.

● What do you need to look out for when you are moving to catch the bubbles?

● What should you do if you accidentally bump into someone?

Aim

To play and move sensibly as a whole class or large group.

Set-up

Grouping:
Whole class together (or smaller groups if you have more adults).

Equipment needed:
Lots of bubble mixture and wands to blow bubbles with.

Space needed:
An outdoor space with a non-slippery surface and not too much wind.

 Cross-curricular link

Why do bubbles go up?
Because the air in our body is warmer than the air outside, the air inside the bubble is warmer and this rises up. (On a hot summer's day, or indoors, the bubbles might not go up!)

23

Aim

To find a partner to work with, to share ideas and to take turns.

Set-up

Grouping:
Pairs or groups of three.

Equipment needed:
One large piece of chalk and one small stone or beanbag per pair or group.

Space needed:
A dry playground surface.

Children could take it in turns to draw the squares on the court.

Hopscotch

Children work together to set up and play this traditional playground game.

How to facilitate the game

1 Draw a hopscotch court.
Bring the class into a large semi-circle with a space in the middle. Draw a simple hopscotch court with numbers in the squares.

2 Demonstrate the game.
Throw a stone or beanbag into one of the numbered boxes, starting with the smallest, closest number. Then move through the court hopping or jumping on each number in order to collect the object and return to the start. If successful, move onto the next highest number on your next turn.

3 Play. 'You are going to work together in pairs or groups of three to design your own hopscotch court and your own way of playing.' Then let the children choose their own groups, collect their own equipment and find their own space.

Adaptations

↑ For older children, the challenge of this game can be increased by designing more complex rules. For example, hopping backwards or moving with eyes closed makes things much trickier.

↑ If you want to spend more time on this activity, different versions of the game can be shared around the class. Each group designs their courts and games, then children move round and play each other's versions. This could be done by having one of the group stay with their court to show how it works, while the others move round.

Assessment for learning

Finding your own partner or group is part of working together. It is worth spending time talking to your class about what you expect of them when they find a partner or group.

● What feelings did you experience when you were looking for a partner?

● What should you do if you can't find a partner to work with?

● What did you like about working with your partner in this game?

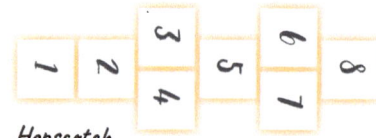

Hopscotch

Cross-curricular link

Hopscotch was a game played by the Romans. The original hopscotch courts were 100 feet long and used for military training routines.

Wall ball

A cooperative batting game, using a ball and a wall.

How to facilitate the game

1 Demonstrate the game. Show the children how to pat the ball against the wall using the palm of the hand. Choose a child to be your partner and take it in turns to pat the ball against the wall. Ensure the children know that this is a cooperative game where you are working together to get the longest rally you can.

2 Play. Tell the class to find a partner and have a go. Ensure the groups are spread out so they all have enough space to play. Any extra children can make a group of three.

Adaptations

↓ For younger children, allow them to catch the ball and throw it back to the wall, rather than pat it back. A larger ball is easier than a smaller one.

↑ For older children, you can offer a choice of rackets or bats. The children could highlight a specific section of the wall that the ball must hit. The children could also turn this into a competitive game, where each player starts with five lives and loses a life with each mistake they make. Mistakes could include missing the ball when trying to hit it back or the ball not reaching the wall when they hit it back.

Assessment for learning

For younger children, use a large, light ball so it is easier to hit and so children get more success. We want them to focus on working together and to consider how best to hit the ball to their partner so it is easy for their partner to hit back.

● Tell your partner how you want them to hit the ball to you.

● Listen to your partner's suggestions and try to adjust how you play to help them succeed.

Aim

To listen to your partner's feedback and make the game easy for your partner to succeed at.

Set-up

Grouping:
Pairs or groups of three.

Equipment needed:
One bouncy ball per group. Optional: an assortment of rackets and bats.

Space needed:
A wall.

Aim

To take turns at leading, and to practise leading an activity.

Set-up

Grouping:
Groups of three.

Equipment needed:
Five different-coloured spots per child.

Space needed:
Any.

Happy feet

A small-group copying activity involving coordination and memory.

How to facilitate the game

1 Demonstrate the game.
Quickly set up three rows of spots, with five different-coloured spots in each row. Ask two children to help you demonstrate; they will each have a row of spots and you will have the third row. Demonstrate a simple movement pattern on your spots. For example, right foot onto blue spot, followed by left foot onto yellow spot. The two children need to watch and then repeat the movement. You then repeat your movement but add an additional step at the end, such as both feet jump onto the green spot. The children watch and repeat. And so on...

2 Play. Ask children to find their own groups of three and set up their spots and areas. It is a good idea to have the groups of five spots already separated out, to avoid a swarm of children all trying to grab spots from the same place at once. If there are children left without a group, they can always join a group to make a group of four or play as a pair instead. Ask the children to ensure everyone in their group gets a turn at leading. You could use a timer for this or you could leave it up to the children to decide when to change the leader.

Adaptations

↑ Once the activity is underway, have a wander around and challenge the leaders to be more creative with their movements. For example, could they do some 180-degree turns and land facing in different directions?

Assessment for learning

PE provides the opportunity to develop confidence in leadership. All children can benefit from being given the chance to lead. Your class will need to be able to share the leadership role over the course of the year.

● How did you make sure everyone got a chance to be the leader?

● What makes a good leader in an activity like this?

Top TIP

If you don't have enough coloured spots to make this activity work for the whole class at once, consider using it as part of a carousel. See page 97 for more information on using the carousel approach.

Hoop trail

A cooperative pair activity involving bouncing a ball in a moving hoop.

How to facilitate the game

1 **Demonstrate the game.** Tie the string onto the hoop like a lead. Ask one child to help you demonstrate and give them a bouncy ball. Place the hoop on the ground and ask the child to bounce their ball inside the hoop. Slowly start moving the hoop so the child needs to move while they are bouncing the ball.

2 **Play.** Ask the children to find a partner, collect their equipment and have a go. Children may need help tying their string so it doesn't break. You could show them how to do this in your demonstration or suggest they 'work together' to do it themselves.

Adaptations

↓ For KS1 children, you could take the ball out of this activity completely, and the child following the hoop needs to jump in and out of the hoop rather than bounce a ball.

This activity will be interesting initially for older children, but it will need some progression to keep their interest. Here are a few suggestions to offer the children, although

they may well have better ones themselves.

↑ How fast can the children go? They should work together to slowly increase speed and reach the fastest speed they can without losing control of the ball.

↑ You could have pairs follow each other. See Follow the Leader (page 159) for ideas on how that could work.

↑ If you have enough space, you could add an element of competition, with pairs of children racing each other or trying to get past some defenders.

Assessment for learning

Some children will find this activity much easier than others. Some will be able to bounce a ball well within a moving hoop, while others may struggle even when the hoop is still. The success of the task will depend on the pair's ability to find a speed that works.

● When you pulled the hoop, how did you know what speed was right for your partner?

● When you were bouncing the ball, how did you let your partner know what speed was right for you?

Aim
To work with a partner to reach your maximum speed.

Set-up

Grouping:
Pairs.

Equipment needed:
One bouncy ball, one hoop and one long piece of string per pair.

Space needed:
Any.

Different-sized hoops and types of ball provide a range of challenge.

Top TIP

Have a variety of different balls available. Some are easier to bounce accurately than others. This allows children to adapt the activity to find something that works for them.

Aim

To work together to choose a game, compete with each other, and to win and lose gracefully.

Set-up

Grouping:
Pairs.

Equipment needed:
A variety, depending on which contests are chosen (see the individual activity pages listed for more details).

Space needed:
Any.

Duels

Pairs of children compete in a variety of one-against-one activities.

How to facilitate the game

1 Introduce the game. Explain to the class that they will be working together in pairs and learning to compete, win and lose, and resolve disputes. It would be a good idea to present these learning intentions on a whiteboard.

2 Demonstrate the duels. Pairs of children can choose between a selection of three or four different duels. Here are some ideas in this book for you to choose from:

a. Floor Ball, page 70
b. Noodle Tag, page 155
c. Cat and Mouse, page 67
d. 1v1 Cone Ball, an adaptation from 2v2 Cone Ball on page 158
e. Arm Tennis, page 174
f. Bib v Ball, page 156
g. Pull Your Weight, page 210
h. Dragon v Shadow, page 134
i. Slam, page 137
j. Noodle fencing, from Pirate Attack on page 212

There's no need for lengthy demonstrations; just explain the basic rules. Have the equipment they need ready. Make it clear that there needs to be a winner of the duel and that when they have finished, they should return their equipment to the equipment area and then find another partner to play against.

3 Play. Let the children choose a partner and a duel and begin. Observe and identify how individual children react to winning and losing. Aim to switch children between pairs and help all children to work with different partners in a variety of duels. Allow the children to experiment with their own rules and scoring.

Assessment for learning

Competition is a key part of the KS1 and KS2 PE National Curriculum. This game provides an opportunity to teach your class how to behave when competing. These questions will start useful conversations with your class about the experience of winning and losing.

- If you lose, how might your opponent behave or what might they say or do which would make it easier for you to accept defeat?

- How might you resolve arguments about the rules or the score?

Cross-curricular link

This activity would be perfect for teaching some important adjectives for KS2: humble, gracious, vanquished, victorious, triumphant, bitter.

Stuck in the mud

A classic whole-class tag game where taggers work together to catch the others.

How to facilitate the game

1 Show the area. In all tag games, the boundaries are important. Make sure these are clearly marked and the children know where they are.

2 Explain the rules. Taggers must try to tag those running away. When a runner is tagged, they stand on the spot in a star shape with their legs and arms apart. They cannot move and are – as the name suggests – stuck in the mud. Those who are tagged can be freed when their teammates run under their outstretched arm. The taggers must try to tag everyone so they are all stuck, while those trying to escape must work together to free their teammates before they all get stuck. For a class of 30 children, about six taggers would be a good number.

3 Play. Choose taggers and begin. Get the game going quickly. Swap taggers regularly. Allow the children to experience the game before and after they discuss the assessment for learning questions.

Adaptations

↑ Introduce safe zones (by marking squares on the floor) where runners can rest for ten seconds without being tagged.

↑ You could make the game directional by introducing chests (indicated by more squares marked on the floor) that are full of treasure (balls), to be guarded by taggers and stolen by the others.

↑ For the very high-ability footballers in the group, those children who really come alive when they have a ball at their feet, challenge them to play while dribbling the ball at the same time.

Assessment for learning

In this game, the taggers can be more successful if they work as a team to catch the runners.

● How could you work together to catch the runners?

● How might you move together to make it hard for the runners to escape?

If you rescue someone who has a ball, then you get the ball (if you want it).

Aim
To work together to chase and trap others in a tag game.

Set-up

Grouping:
Whole class together.

Equipment needed:
Bibs to denote taggers.
Optional: a number of large balls.

Space needed:
This game can work in a small hall as well as a large playground. A large space needs more taggers than a small space.

Top TIP
Be careful when playing this game in a very large area, as this will lead to lots of standing still, interspersed by longer-distance, high-speed chases – which may end in dangerous collisions. A smaller area will add intensity and require many more starts, stops and changes of direction.

Treasure tag

A whole-class tag game in two teams.

Aim

To work together to devise tactics and communicate while competing.

Set-up

Grouping:
Whole class together.

Equipment needed:
A coloured bib for every child – half of these bibs should be in one colour and the other half in a contrasting colour (for example, yellow and red); ten small pieces of treasure, each piece small enough to be held in a clenched fist (dice are ideal, but small stones would also work).

Space needed:
Any.

How to facilitate the game

1 Show the area. Show children the boundaries of the playing area.

2 Divide the class into two teams of approximately even numbers. One half of the class wear yellow bibs tucked into their waistband or pocket and the others wear red bibs.

3 Explain the rules. To start with it is a simple tag game, where the two teams try to pinch a bib from an opponent. If someone manages to pinch a bib, they take it to the side of the playing area. The player who lost the bib should retrieve it and re-join the game.

4 Play. Have a go at this game first to get used to the area and the rules.

5 Add in the treasure. Now you are going to give each team five pieces of small treasure.

They must distribute the treasure across the players in their team, so five different players are holding a piece of treasure each. They hold the treasure in their clenched fist so no one can see it. During the game, each team tries to steal the other team's treasure. The winning team is the first team to get all ten pieces of treasure. This is how the children can steal treasure from the other team:

- If someone is tagged in the game and has their bib stolen, they must retrieve it from the side of the area as before.

- Before tucking their bib back in, they must show their two fists to the person who tagged them.

- The person who tagged them can select one of their fists to open. If the treasure is there, they may take it.

Treasure is allowed to be passed between players on the same team at any time during the game.

Top TIP

With complicated or complex games, consider starting the game with a simplified version first. Then add in the more complex rules after the children have got used to the game. It is also worth considering replaying the game again in a future lesson to give children time to digest how it works and how to be successful.

Adaptations

↓ This game may be too complicated for some KS1 classes. You should consider taking away the treasure element of the game to start with and only adding it in once you think the class is ready.

↓ You could have three or four (or more!) smaller teams instead of two big ones, all playing at once. The smaller team size might make it easier for team members to discuss tactics and ideas together.

Assessment for learning

To be successful, children will need to deceive their opponents by pretending they have treasure when they don't, and vice versa. They should work this out themselves but it could be worth spending time on the first question below to share understanding. The second question aims to get children thinking about how they work together to protect the treasure they have.

● How do you make it hard for the other team to know who has the treasure?

● How might you try to protect teammates who have the treasure?

Steal an opponent's bib, choose a fist and if you find treasure – it's yours!

 Aim

To work together with your teammates and opponents to play a competitive team game fairly and resolve any issues yourselves.

Set-up

Grouping:
Teams of three to five.

Equipment needed:
One frisbee per game.

Space needed:
Three or four small-sided pitches with 'end zones' (see page xvii for examples of how this might be set up).

Ultimate

A small-sided, frisbee-throwing invasion game for Key Stage 2.

How to facilitate the game

1 Show the pitch. Make sure the children can see the two end zones.

2 Explain the rules. The frisbee should be thrown and caught between players on a team. A point is scored if the team catches the frisbee in the end zone at the end of the pitch they are attacking.

- Players can't run with the frisbee and they can't grab it from each other.

- If the frisbee is thrown and drops onto the floor without being caught then possession changes to the other team.

- Players have ten seconds to throw the frisbee and this can be counted down by the opposing players.

3 Play. Remind the class that the focus is on working together. Ask them how they might resolve any conflicts that arise during the game. Then send teams to the pitches to begin their game.

Adaptations

↓ Competitive games can be tricky for many children in PE, especially for those with lower confidence, motivation, game understanding or game ability. As you observe the games being played, identify the teams that are performing at the highest and lowest levels. You can then switch teams to make games more equal if needed.

↓ For lower KS2 classes, try smaller team sizes (two or three children per team) and use an object that is easy to throw and catch. A bib tied in a knot is good as it is easy to grab while being heavy enough to throw.

Assessment for learning

These kinds of game will almost certainly include disputes around rules and fairness. This is part of the learning experience for the children and presents an important opportunity to teach.

- How could you quickly resolve any disputes you have in a game like this?

- What should you do if you notice one of your teammates breaking the rules?

Classroom debate

'Strict rules are very important in PE games.' Do you agree or disagree?

Cooperative learning

PE provides a valuable opportunity to develop cooperation and collaboration skills. The cooperative learning approach could help teachers to organise and structure PE so that children can practise supporting and helping each other.

Why?

The cooperative learning approach is useful because it engages children in their own learning and recognises the value of peer collaboration in the learning process. When we teach children to seek help from others or to share their own understanding in order to teach others, we help them to practise valuable learning routines and processes. The small group set-up and the focus on problem-solving fits well for the exploration of games in primary PE.

What?

Cooperative learning is a term used to describe a range of approaches to teaching and learning that provide children with ownership and responsibility for their own learning. Cooperative learning typically arranges children in small groups to explore an activity, before providing opportunities for sharing understanding and teaching each other.

The five elements of cooperative learning in PE, below, are taken from Dyson and Casey's book, *Cooperative Learning in Physical Education and Physical Activity* (2016).

1 Children need to interact and rely on each other in order to complete and succeed at the task.

2 Children spend time physically close to each other and support each other with positive dialogue and positive feedback.

3 Each child takes responsibility for completing their part of the task for their group.

4 Children practise listening, shared decision-making, taking responsibility, giving and receiving feedback, leading, following and encouraging each other.

5 Children process and reflect on tasks through discussion which they guide, facilitated rather than led by the teacher.

How?

- Games should be chosen so they have a common goal or pursue an agreed outcome.

- Children should then be organised into small groups in order to explore the activity (ideally groups of three or four children). Groups should be heterogenous, so should be a mixture of sexes, ethnicities, abilities and so on. It is a good idea to keep groups constant for several lessons in order to give them a chance to develop effective working relationships.

- The teacher should assign specific tasks so that each child is responsible for some part of the learning process.

- Once the game has been explored, there are various ways in which learning and understanding can be shared. See page 188 for some of the many ways to facilitate group sharing and learning.

See Beanbag Golf (page 34) for an example of the cooperative learning approach in action.

More information

- Dyson, B. and Casey, A. (2016), *Cooperative Learning in Physical Education and Physical Activity: A practical introduction*. Abingdon: Routledge.
- On YouTube, search 'Cooperative Learning in Physical Education, Ashley Casey' for a wonderful playlist of short, simple videos on cooperative learning.

Aim

To explore working as a team and following rules.

Set-up

Grouping:
Teams of three or four.

Equipment needed:
Four or five hula hoops and tall cones, and one beanbag per team. Optional: a whiteboard or paper to record scores.

Space needed:
An interesting play area.

Beanbag golf

This game uses the cooperative learning approach to explore following rules and working with others.

How to facilitate the game

1 Prepare the teams. In cooperative learning, teams should be a mix of different abilities, sexes and ethnicities. Try not to group best friends or enemies together.

2 Set up the holes. Unless you have time before your lesson, use a quick starter game to occupy the children while you set up at least four or five different 'holes'. Each hole needs to start with a tall cone – from which the first throw is taken – and end in a hoop. (Alternatively, you could give each team a cone and hoop and ask them to help you set up a range of different holes.)

3 Demonstrate the game. Bring the children in to where they can easily see one hole. Choose two children to be in your team and show the rest of the class how to take it in turns to throw the beanbag and how to keep score. Explain that the aim is to work together to get the beanbag into the hoop in as few throws as possible, but you must take it in turns to throw. The team has a collective score, e.g. they score four points if it has taken them four throws to get the beanbag through the hoop.

4 Give the tasks. Each member of the team will be accountable for answering one of the following questions. Assign these questions before the game and ask the children to think about their answers while they play. They will then discuss their answers in groups after the game. (See the assessment for learning section for more details.)

a. What makes a good team?
b. Why do we have rules? Why might people break them?
c. How do you resolve disputes in a team?
d. How can teammates best support each other?

5 Play. Once the children are ready you can send them to one of the holes to begin. Teams can then move round so they play on a variety of different holes.

Adaptations

If you have time, teams could repeat some holes, aiming to beat their previous score.

⬆ For KS2 children, you could replace the beanbag with a frisbee if you wanted a different challenge.

Assessment for learning

Use the 'numbered heads together' method to share ideas and understanding between the teams. With each child assigned a different question to explore during the game (see point four in 'How to facilitate the game'), you can now group children from different teams together based on the question they explored and give them time to discuss their thoughts. This could be effective as a classroom activity and you could give each group a piece of flipchart paper. You could even ask groups to present their thoughts to the class afterwards.

You could offer further questions during this process. For example, for the group discussing rules:

● How does it feel when other people break the rules?

● What should we do when we are tempted to break the rules? What about when a teammate is breaking the rules?

Why might people cheat?

● I wanted to win!
● It was too difficult!
● I didn't know the rules!
● Someone else broke the rules first!
● My rules are better!

All these responses provide important teaching opportunities.

National Curriculum links

KS1 and KS2:
'Embed values of fairness, respect and kindness.'

Children help get things ready for their PE lesson. This responsibility offers a chance to teach and learn about helping each other and having respect for equipment.

October

Thinking of others

An introduction to thinking of others

Learning in October builds on last month's 'working together' theme. We continue to work on fairness and taking it in turns, but we also focus on the social skills of being respectful and including others. By the end of the month, we should aim for all children to be able to work kindly with their classmates.

Some of the games this month are designed to encourage children to consider how they use the rules of the games to help others. Superpower Tag (page 53) and Hoop Buzz (page 42) involve children making decisions in games which recognise the needs of others. Teachers should positively reinforce examples of cooperation and inclusion.

PE offers the chance to deliberately work on values such as kindness and respect. It is a good idea to begin work on a 'class agreement' during October, a simple pact that sets out the rules and expectations of how children behave with each other. This could be co-created with the children, and perhaps linked to the school's values or whole-school improvement plan. You could print this out to remind children of what they have agreed. The activities this month provide essential opportunities to discuss what these behaviours look like in action.

'How to...' pages this month focus on scoring systems, choosing teams and including children with special educational needs and disabilities (SEND) in PE.

Key skills

- Being patient and respectful with each other
- Recognising and embracing difference
- Noticing when someone needs help in a game
- Using the rules of the game to help teammates
- Helping each other to improve and encouraging each other
- Appreciating the help of others
- Making sure we include everyone
- Adjusting activities so everyone can be involved

Ten top tips for including children with SEND in PE

Approximately one in seven children in state-funded primary schools in England have special educational needs, according to 2020/21 statistics from the Department for Education (https://explore-education-statistics.service.gov.uk). Every child is unique, so there is no single, magic solution for including children with SEND in PE lessons. However, these tips offer help to make PE a successful experience for children with SEND.

1 **Read and know their support plan.** Children with SEND should have a statement or plan in place to help support them. Consider how the information in this plan relates to the context of PE.

2 **Talk to the child and their family** about their needs. Keep a continued dialogue going, so the child can let you know how it's going for them.

3 **Find out about their condition or context** in relation to your PE environment. This may include doing some research online or talking to people in your school who have more knowledge or experience.

4 **Build the relationship.** Take time, in PE and outside of PE, to get to know the child.

5 **Talk to the class** about how they can help support the needs of all children in PE. Ask permission from the child and their family if you think it would be beneficial to discuss that child's particular needs with the class. This can be powerful, as it helps the child's classmates understand how they can help.

6 **Focus on what the child *can* do** and build upon this. Dial down the pressure and be patient and realistic with progress. Allow choice of equipment and role.

7 **Plan your PE lessons with adaptations to activities.** The STEP framework (see page 61) can help you think about how to adapt games. Consider having a 'safe place' in your physical environment – somewhere people can go to take time out if they need some quiet time.

8 **Include a range of cooperative activities.** For example, in Hoop Buzz (page 42) or Noodle Rounders (page 50), there is a focus on everyone helping each other to achieve.

9 **Use support staff to manage lessons** if possible, and plan and review with support staff before and after lessons.

10 **Reflect and find things that work.** Remember that every child is unique. There is no single solution that works for every condition or disability.

Four ways to choose teams for games

Teachers need to consider how to choose teams for games so the process is efficient and respectful. It is not acceptable to line everyone up and have captains pick their classmates one by one. Not only is this a big time-waster, but it also lowers the self-esteem of the poor children who are left at the end.

It can take a lengthy period of the lesson for the teacher to put the children into teams one child at a time. To avoid this, you could let the children choose their own teams. They will typically choose friendship groups, and sometimes this works well. However, when you want to encourage children to work with those they don't usually interact with, you could use one of the following ideas.

1 Make a group of...

'Make a group of... seven!' Children need to work together to get into a huddle of seven as quickly as possible. Then quickly add a new number: 'Now, make a group of three!' Then, finally: 'Make a group of five!' You now have five-a-side teams, which should be a bit of a mixture of friendship groups.

2 Use literacy or numeracy groups from the classroom

This is quick, efficient, and will likely lead to groups of mixed abilities. Children are working in the same groups as they do in the classroom, which is good for familiarity and for potential PE review discussions back in their seats. On the other hand, children may want a break from their usual groups.

3 Use a social hook

For example, 'I'll give you 20 seconds to find someone else in the class who has the same (or a similar) house or flat number as you.' Or, 'Find someone who had the same thing as you for breakfast this morning.' Or, 'Find someone with the same number of brothers and sisters as you.' Then join pairs together into teams.

4 Scarf toss

Start the lesson with this quick starter game from page 65. Use a carefully selected number of different-coloured scarfs or bibs. Swap partners a couple of times during the game. When you stop the game, whichever colour scarf or bib you are holding is your team.

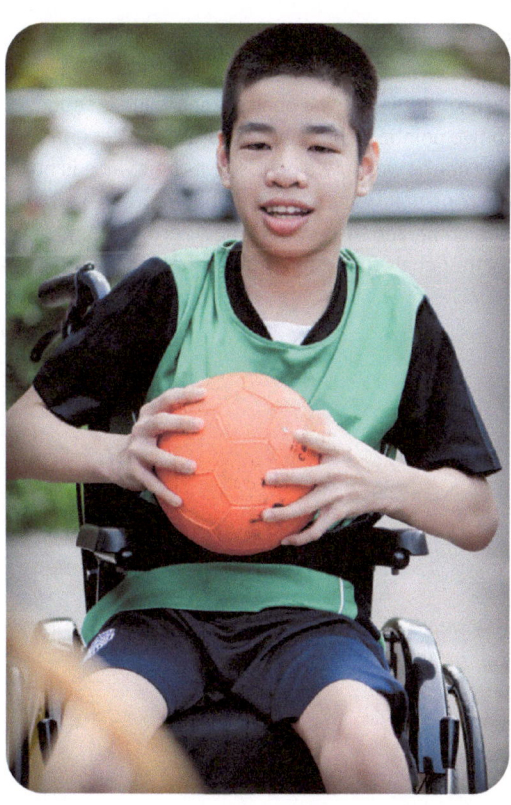

Four inclusive scoring systems for invasion games

In Team Ball on page 55, we use a special scoring system that encourages the children to include each other in order to gain more points. Here are four other scoring systems for inclusion in invasion games.

1 The autograph game

To win the game, everyone on your team must score a goal (or point or basket, depending on what you are playing). Write the name of everyone on your team on a whiteboard. Each time someone scores, they run over to the whiteboard and put a tick next to their name. The first team to tick everyone off wins.

2 3-2-1!

Each player starts the game with a value of three points. When they score a goal, their team gets three points – but the goalscorer's value is reduced to two points. If that player scores another goal, this goal is worth two points, but their value is now only one point. The next goal they score is worth one point, and their value is now zero – so any further goals they score don't count.

3 Star player

Each player keeps their own score. They get a point for every goal they score. They get ten points for each different teammate they 'assist' or set up to score (an assist is when you help a teammate score a goal or point by passing them the ball when you are near the goal or basket). At the end of the game, the winning team is the one that has the player with the highest score.

4 Share the goals

If you score a goal, you can't score your team's next goal. This simple rule helps to share the goalscoring around the team. A child who has scored a goal needs to focus on helping a teammate to score next.

Funky dance tag

A whole-class tag game with lashings of creativity and variety.

How to facilitate the game

1 Explain the game. Tell the class that they are going to play a tag game. If they get caught by the taggers, they must freeze and do a funky dance on the spot. One of their teammates can rescue them if they come over and copy the funky dance for ten seconds.

2 Choose five taggers (for a class of 30). You can easily adjust this later by adding more taggers if you see that the runners are finding it too easy to escape. Taggers can be identified by wearing a bib or holding their hand on their head, or maybe they have to make a funny noise or move in a particular way – be creative!

3 Play. Swap the taggers after a while. You don't need to stop the activity when you do this. Just call a tagger and a runner over to you and ask them to swap roles.

Assessment for learning

Most young children in a tag game will focus almost exclusively on not getting caught by the taggers. We want them to start to consider their teammates and notice when someone has been caught and needs rescuing.

● How many different funky dances did you do?

● How did you choose who to rescue?

● When is a good time to rescue someone?

Aim

To notice when a classmate needs help.

Set-up

Grouping:
Whole class together.

Equipment needed:
None.

Space needed:
Any.

Top TIP

If you are short of space, add this rule: taggers can only tag the runners on the back. This will make it harder for the taggers and give the runners a chance to escape even in a small area. (This adaptation is useful for all tag games.)

Aim

To understand that we all have different needs and to amend the difficulty level to include others.

Set-up

Grouping:
Pairs or groups of three.

Equipment needed:
One hoop per group.

Space needed:
Any.

Knee-height is a good height to start at.

Hoop buzz

Children challenge each other in this electrifying hoop game.

How to facilitate the game

1 **Demonstrate the game.** Ask two children to help you demonstrate. The two children hold a hoop between them at waist height, one on either side. Make a point of showing that the hoop is electric, by feigning a shock and making a 'Buzz!' sound when you touch the hoop. Demonstrate stepping forward into the hoop and then stepping forward out of the hoop again without touching the electric hoop.

2 **Adjust the challenge.** Ask the children: what could the pair holding the hoop do if it is too difficult for the one stepping in and out? What could they do if it is too easy? If it is not clear to the children, you could show them how the pair of children holding the hoop can adjust the height of the hoop to find the right level of challenge.

3 **Play.** Ask the children to take turns at being the one who steps in and out of the hoop. Ask them to make sure that the level is just right for each person so it is not too easy and not too hard.

Adaptations

↑ The child stepping into the hoop has a beanbag on their head. They must step into the hoop without the beanbag falling.

↑ The children could crawl under the hoop to begin with and climb in from below before stepping out. You could encourage children to find their own ways to get in and out of the hoop.

Assessment for learning

Young children may have difficulty judging each other's competency and working with those who aren't as competent in an activity as they are. PE provides the perfect opportunity to help them understand that we all have a different set of abilities and that we can help include each other better by changing activities to make them easier or harder.

● How did you know what height to hold the hoop at?

● What did you do if the hoop was too easy or too difficult to step into?

● Why is it important in PE that we change our games so everyone can find the right level for them? Is there another PE game that we could change in this way?

 **Cross-curricular link**

Electricity travels at the speed of light, which is more than 186,000 miles per second. One flash of lightning could power 1,000 houses for a whole year.

Down the rabbit hole

A pair activity involving throwing and rolling.

How to facilitate the game

1 Demonstrate the game.
Ask for two children to help you demonstrate. One child has a hula hoop and rolls it out into the middle of the area. Once the hoop has settled on the floor, the other child tries to throw a beanbag (the rabbit) so the beanbag lands inside the hoop (the rabbit hole). They score a point if they can do so. If you have enough beanbags then the children could have three throws per roll of the hoop.

2 Play. Don't bother giving the children any technical information about throwing at this stage. If needed, you can correct their techniques later once you have seen what they can do.

Adaptations

The aim of this activity is to practise working together but alternatively it could be used to explore the fundamental movement skills of throwing and sending.

↑ You can switch around the order, so the beanbag is thrown first and then the hoop is rolled with the aim of landing around the beanbag. This makes the game more difficult. You could also experiment with different ways of rolling the hoop and of throwing the beanbag.

Assessment for learning

This is a fun but challenging task that can form the basis of discussions around appreciation and encouragement.

● What did your partner do or say that was helpful?

● When do you think people find praise or encouragement most useful?

Aim

To appreciate help from your partner and to use praise and encouragement.

Set-up

Grouping:
Pairs.

Equipment needed:
One hoop and one object (a beanbag is ideal) per pair.

Space needed:
Any.

Cross-curricular link

The phrase 'down the rabbit hole' comes from Lewis Carroll's 1865 book Alice's Adventures in Wonderland. *The phrase is used to describe someone falling or descending into a complex or difficult state or situation.*

A netball court is already divided into three areas, so it is a perfect set-up for small games, with one game taking place in each rectangular third of the court.

Top TIP

Be careful using games where bibs are thrown onto a slippery floor. This game works best on a playground surface rather than an indoor hall.

Spiderman

A throwing and dodging game played in small teams.

Aim

To keep an eye out for frozen teammates who need rescuing.

How to facilitate the game

1 Show the area. Get the children into a position where they can all see the area where you will be demonstrating. Split the court in two by making a short line of spots or cones along the middle (or use an existing line on the playground).

2 Demonstrate the game. Choose eight children to help you demonstrate and put them into two teams of four. Ask each team to stand on one side of the line and explain that they are not allowed to cross over the line, so they have to stay on their own side. Place four or five bibs on the line.

3 Explain the rules. The bibs will be the 'webs', which children can pick up and throw at the other team. If someone on the other team gets hits with a web, they are 'frozen' and must stand on one leg and await rescue. The winning team is the first one to get all children on the other team frozen at once. Those who are frozen can be unfrozen by catching a bib. This could be a bib thrown by someone on the opposite team or from one of their teammates.

4 Play. Children can choose teams and begin. Alternatively, see page 39 for methods you can use to put children into teams.

Adaptations

⬆ Each team has one person assigned in the role of Elektra, who is one of Spiderman's friends. Elektra is the only one who can rescue her frozen teammates (by throwing a bib for them to catch), and she has superpowers, which means she can't be frozen herself. Teachers who notice a child who doesn't seem so included might try giving them the role of Elektra.

⬆ A useful additional rule is: if a child catches a bib thrown by an opponent, the child who threw the bib freezes and the one who caught the bib does not.

⬆ To turn this into a main game, you could add tennis balls or beanbags at either end of the court and progress into Capture the Flag (page 161).

Assessment for learning

When someone picks up a bib from the floor, the most exciting thing is to throw it over the line to try to hit an opponent. However, the children also need to recognise that they could use the bib to rescue a frozen teammate.

● How did you decide what to do with a bib?

● How does it feel when you are frozen?

● What does kindness look like in this game?

Set-up

Grouping:
Groups of six to eight.

Equipment needed:
Enough bibs for half the children to have one, and markers or cones to make a line on the floor.

Space needed:
Three pitches for a class of 30. (See page xvii for an example of how this is set up.)

Aim

To practise being patient with each other.

Set-up

Grouping:
Groups of three or four.

Equipment needed:
One long skipping rope per group.

Space needed:
You will need eight long ropes for a class of 30, with space between each group so the rope can swing without hitting adjacent groups. So, a large space is needed if you want all children to be involved at once.

Group skipping

A collaborative long-rope skipping activity to practise coordination and timing.

How to facilitate the game

1 Demonstrate the rope swing. Choose a partner to help you. Hold one end of the rope each. Stand apart from each other and see if you can get the rope to swing in circles, high and low.

2 Demonstrate the game. Choose a child who would like to try and jump the rope. The volunteer should position themselves in the middle of the two rope swingers, facing towards one of them. The easiest way to start skipping is for the rope to begin on the floor at the side of the jumper and begin by swinging it up and over their head. See if the volunteer can time their jumps so they jump over the rope.

3 Play. You have set the challenge. Now let the children find groups, get a rope, look for a space, and have a go themselves. Groups should count how many successful jumps they can make in a row. If you have a group of four, you can have two children jumping at once.

Adaptations

This can also work with just two children by tying one end of the rope to a fence or railing and having one child hold the other end and swing it.

↓ If you have enough adults, it might work better for young children if the adults hold the rope and make it swing. If you go with this option then don't have all the class line up and wait their turn. Instead, give them a skipping rope each and ask them to practise their skipping and call a pair of children over one at a time to have a turn with the adults.

↑ For those children who can skip well, challenge them to start outside the rope area, run into the swinging rope and start jumping in time with the swing.

Assessment for learning

This is a difficult task, even for older children. Children may become frustrated with each other, and this provides opportunities for important teaching around how we remain patient with each other while we practise.

● What were the most difficult things to get right in this game?

● How might other people have felt when they got things wrong?

● How does being patient with each other help us practise together?

It is easier for jumpers to time their jumps if they face one of the swingers.

Top TIP

There are really useful possibilities here to link PE learning to playtime and lunchtime activity. The children have learnt a physical activity they can now design and play for themselves. Have skipping ropes available at breaktimes.

 Aim

To work out ways
to help other people
to succeed.

 Set-up

Grouping:
Whole class together
(or in smaller groups).

Equipment needed:
Five bibs to denote
taggers are useful.
A selection of balls
to travel with is optional.

Space needed:
Any.

Cross the lake

A whole-class or small-group tag game with a focus on movement decisions in crowded areas.

How to facilitate the game

1 Show the area. This game is typically played in a large square or rectangle (the lake). Sit the children somewhere where they can see the boundaries of the lake.

2 Demonstrate the game. Use a whiteboard to show how the game works. Draw the lake on the whiteboard and add in some crocodiles to the middle of the area. The crocodiles will be the taggers. For a class of 30 children, four or five crocodiles is a good number to start with. Everyone else is a fish and they start on any of the four sides of the lake. Draw a fish onto the whiteboard and draw a line to show how they might get across the lake while avoiding the crocodiles.

3 Play. Choose which children will be crocodiles and ask the fish to go to the side they'd like to start on. When the crocodiles are ready, you can begin. If a fish is tagged by a crocodile, the fish returns to the side of the lake and tries again. Try the game for a few minutes until everyone has got the hang of how it works.

4 Progress. You need to find a way of switching the crocodiles every so often and one neat way is to say that crocodiles need to change places with the third fish they tag. Points can be awarded to each fish for different ways of getting across the lake. For example, it could be a point for getting to the other side without being tagged. You might add in additional points for travelling with a ball or moving between two crocodiles. As the learning intention is about including everyone, you could add in additional points for helping someone else get across the lake.

Adaptations

You could divide the class to work in smaller groups (using smaller lakes with one or two crocodiles). If you do this, then demonstrate the game with one group before sending the other groups to their area to play. This is a useful set-up to encourage children to invent their own rules and points scoring system.

↑ In order to maintain intensity for older children, you could add in a rule that if everyone is stood still on the sides of the lake without moving, the crocodiles can change places with anyone they like.

Assessment for learning

It will be interesting to see how children try to help each other to get across the lake. For younger children, you may suggest possible ways, like holding hands with someone less confident or distracting the crocodiles to make

Smaller squares with one shark in each square. This set-up encourages groups of children to create their own rules and ways of playing.

some space for others. With older children, you can help share ideas with the following questions.

- How did you recognise someone who was struggling to cross the lake?

- What might you do to help a fish who keeps getting caught by the crocodiles?

- What kind of help did you get from a classmate which was useful?

Classroom debate

Which is more important in PE: kindness or respect?

Aim

To throw the ball to each other so it's easy to catch.

Set-up

Grouping:
Teams of four or five.

Equipment needed:
Each pitch will need a tall cone, a noodle, a soft ball, and an end line or end cone to denote where batters need to run to.

Space needed:
Each pitch will host two teams playing against each other. Pitches can be small and overlap (see page xvii for a useful set-up).

Noodle rounders

It's a race between batters and fielders in this small-sided striking game.

How to facilitate the game

1 Show the area. On each pitch, there is a tall cone at the batting area, with a ball balanced on top. There is an end zone about five to ten metres away.

2 Explain the batters' role. The batter must bat the ball off the cone using a noodle, so the ball goes into the playing area. After that, the batter must run to the end cone and come back and tag the next batter in their team, and so on. The batting team gets a point for every batter who runs to the end cone and back. Choose four children to be the batting team and ask them to go and get ready.

3 Explain the fielders' role. The nearest fielder needs to get the ball as it is batted into the playing area. The fielders then are not allowed to move and they must stand still exactly where they are. The fielder who has the ball must throw it to another fielder and then sit down. That fielder must throw the ball to another fielder and then sit down, and so on. Once all the fielders are sat down, the batters can no longer run. It may be useful to add a rule that states the fielders must be at least three big steps away from each other. Choose four children to be the fielding team and ask them to go into the playing area.

4 Demonstrate the game in action by asking the first batter to have a hit. Make sure the children have understood the rules.

5 Play. Put the other children into teams and send them to their areas to begin. After everyone has had two bats each, change batters and fielders.

Adaptations

↓ For KS1 classes, this game could work as a three-a-side game to keep everyone more involved. You could also move the end cone nearer to the tall cone so the batters don't have to run so far.

↑ You could insist on a completed throw and catch before the fielder sits down, so they have to repeat the action if the ball is dropped.

Assessment for learning

In this game, the children's ability to throw and catch is put under pressure by having to do it quickly. This means they sometimes forget to be considerate when they throw the ball and do so too quickly for their teammate to catch it.

● How would you want the ball to arrive to you so you can catch it easily?

● Why might it actually be quicker to throw the ball more slowly and carefully?

Top TIP

Please don't play this as one large whole-class game! The children spend almost the entire lesson standing around waiting to be involved. Make the effort to get this going as three or four small-sided games instead.

Aim

To include your partner (or the other players) on your team.

Set-up

Grouping:
Pairs or teams of three.

Equipment needed:
One soft, bouncy ball per game. A 'net', which could be a bench, some cones or a line on the floor.

Space needed:
Courts should be small so there isn't too much room to score a point on either side of the net. For a class of 30, you'll need six courts to host a variety of two-a-side and three-a-side games.

Sitting volleyball

A competitive 'net or wall' game on a small court.

How to facilitate the game

1 Demonstrate the game. Choose six children to come and demonstrate the game in two teams of three and sit one team down either side of the net (or you could play in pairs). Explain that you score a point if you throw the ball over the net so it lands on the floor of the opponents' side. Each team is allowed one pass on their own side of the court before sending the ball over the net. Do a quick demonstration. It is probably easiest for children to play in a kneeling position.

2 Play. Tell the children to find a team and a court.

Adaptations

↓ For younger children, you can slow this game down by using a balloon instead. If you fill the balloon with a small amount of rice, it will be a bit heavier and make a really cool sound.

↑ For older children, you could adapt the rules so each team *must* pass it once on their side of the net. However, this pass cannot be caught. Instead, it must be batted over the net without catching it.

Assessment for learning

This challenge will work best if you are able to mix the teams around so friendship groups are split up and children need to work with others they don't typically play with. These questions will help reflect on why it's important to include all the team members.

- How does it feel when no one passes to you in a game?

- Why is it important in team games that we include everyone to be successful?

Cross-curricular link

Sitting volleyball was first invented as a way of helping injured soldiers recover after the Second World War. It started as a Paralympic sport in 1980.

Superpower tag

A whole-class tag game with a throwing and catching theme.

How to facilitate the game

1 Explain the game. Tell the class they are going to play a tag game and show them the area that the game will be played in.

2 Choose six taggers who will try to tag the rest of the children. You could ask the taggers to wear bibs so everyone knows who they are. Alternatively, the taggers must hold one hand on their head at all times and use the other hand to tag.

3 Introduce the balls. Tell the class that whoever is holding a ball has a superpower and cannot be tagged. Give the non-taggers five balls and tell them they can pass the balls between them. Also add the key rule that if someone is tagged, they must freeze and can be released when they catch a ball thrown to them by a teammate.

4 Play. Let the children have a turn to play. It may take a while for them to understand how best to use the balls to protect each other. Let them have a few turns at the game, changing the taggers each time.

Adaptations

↓ For younger children, play a normal tag game first before introducing the superpower objects. They don't have to be objects that are thrown and caught; they could be objects that are simply given from one child to another.

↑ For older children, this game can also be played with the taggers only able to tag people who do have a ball. This makes the game harder for the taggers and also introduces more urgency into the passing of the ball.

Assessment for learning

Some children will want to keep hold of the ball as it provides them with a superpower. However, they need to recognise others who are more in need of this protection, as well as recognising their own role of releasing tagged teammates when they have the ball.

● When you have the ball, how do you know who needs it more than you do?

● How does 'thinking of others' help you in this game?

Aim

To consider how to use the superpower to protect others.

Set-up

Grouping:
Whole class together.

Equipment needed:
Five objects that can be thrown and caught – this could be a variety of different sizes and shapes of balls. Optional: six bibs to denote taggers.

Space needed:
Any.

A netball court can be split into three
to create three small-sided pitches.

Team ball

A small-sided variation of handball for Key Stage 2 designed to encourage inclusion.

How to facilitate the game

1 Show the pitch. Set up the pitches and put children into teams (by handing out bibs if you're using them) while the children are enjoying a quick starter game. Bring the children in so they can all see one of the pitches. Show them that the pitch has an end zone at each end.

2 Demonstrate the game. Choose three children to be on your team. Show the class how you can throw and catch the ball between you, and how you score by running the ball into the end zone or throwing to someone who is in the end zone. The key rule that they need to know is that if a child is tagged while they are moving with the ball in their hands, they lose possession to the child who tagged them. But if they are not moving, they cannot be tagged. They can start and stop moving with the ball as many times as they like. Children are not allowed to grab the ball from each other.

3 Play. Let the children have a turn to play. You may need to revisit some of last month's work on resolving disputes (see page 21).

4 Introduce the scoring. The scoring system is designed for inclusive team play, and teams that pass to everyone on their team will do the best on the scoreboard. Each goal scored is worth the number of passes in the build-up to the goal, multiplied by three if everyone on the team has touched the ball. Whoever scores is responsible for running over to the whiteboard to record their score, and the game carries on while they do this.

Assessment for learning

The following questions ask the children to consider why we need to include everyone in games.

- How did the scoring system encourage you to include all the players on your team?
- Can you think of a team sport where you need to trust and include all the players on your team in order to do well?

Top TIP

Getting the pitches and teams organised while the children are all actively engaged in a quick starter game is a good use of time. You can distribute coloured bibs to children while they are involved in Hoop Buzz (page 42) or Group Skipping (page 46), for example, and they will all then be ready for when you want to start.

Aim

To include everyone on your team in game play.

Set-up

Grouping:
Teams of four or five.

Equipment needed:
One ball per pitch. A whiteboard and pen at the side of each pitch to record the score. Optional: coloured bibs for teams.

Space needed:
For a class of 30, three pitches are perfect. Each pitch needs an end zone at each end. (See page xvii for an example set-up.)

National Curriculum links

KS1:
'Pupils should engage in competitive (against self)... physical activities in a range of increasingly challenging situations.'

KS2:
'Pupils should be taught to demonstrate improvement to achieve their personal best.'

November

Challenging yourself

An introduction to challenging yourself

Learning in November focuses on the attitudes, skills and interactions needed to 'beat your own score' or 'achieve your personal best' – and to support others to do the same. Games like Cat and Mouse (page 67) encourage children to challenge themselves individually, and these skills are explored in pairs in Scarf Toss Challenge (page 65) and in teams in Knights and Castles (page 71).

One of the aims this month is to make children responsible for adjusting PE tasks to suit their own level of confidence and perceived ability. The STEP model on page 61 could usefully be taught to older children to provide a framework for doing this. In addition, teachers are advised to consider how they can design or modify games so they are realistic, relevant and challenging by adding defenders, movement, direction and choice (see page 58 for more details).

Teaching in November may explore how feelings (like excitement, focus, boredom and anxiety) change when we amend the level of difficulty of the task in relation to own perceived ability level. November is a good month to begin finding out about the children's feelings and experiences in PE and several possible methods for this purpose are explored on page 62.

Key skills

- Making a task more difficult
- Creating and using a scale of different difficulty levels
- Measuring a personal best score and demonstrating improvement
- Being brave and trying something more difficult
- Challenging yourself in a competitive game
- Achieving a personal best as an individual and within a team game
- Recognising how being challenged affects feelings, confidence and motivation
- Supporting each other to choose more difficult options

Floor Ball (page 70).

Making games more challenging

The flow zone

Flow is the 'state in which people are so involved in an activity that they are completely absorbed and nothing else seems to matter' (Csikszentmihalyi, 1990).

Children's experience of a game will be largely influenced by the relationship between their own skill level (and perceived skill level) and the level of challenge of the task. This relationship will be different for each child and in each game. We need to find ways of helping all children into the flow zone by encouraging them to adjust their own games.

Here are some useful questions to consider with children. Perhaps reflect on the first two questions before showing them the graph:

1 In PE, how does it feel when a task is too easy/difficult for you?

2 In PE, how do you know when a task is too easy/difficult for you?

3 In PE, what could you do to move yourself into the flow zone?

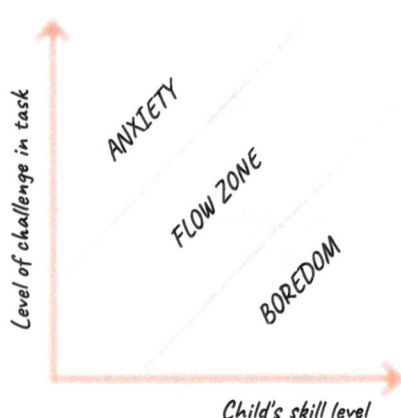

The concentration face: an indicator that the child is achieving the right level of challenge.

More information

● Csikszentmihalyi, M. (1990), *Flow: The psychology of optimal experience*. New York, NY: Harper Perennial.

Playing a *real* game

Even young children are capable of playing games where they need to make decisions and face the kind of challenges they would in a real game. The skill of the teacher is in dialling this level of challenge up and down so children are challenged at an appropriate level. Here are a few options for how to add decision-making, choice, movement and direction to a simple 'unopposed' game.

Here are two children throwing and catching a ball between them.

This activity is 'unopposed' – i.e. there is no one trying to stop them, or no defenders.

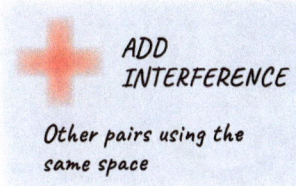

ADD INTERFERENCE

Other pairs using the same space

This adds decision-making, e.g. when to throw the ball so it doesn't collide.

ADD A DEFENDER

E.g. 'piggy in the middle'

The activity is now 'opposed' – someone is trying to stop them.

ADD MORE DEFENDERS

Two against two, increase team size

This could be described as a small-sided game.

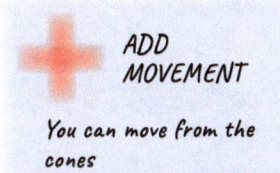

ADD MOVEMENT

You can move from the cones

This adds decision-making, e.g. where to move to after you have thrown.

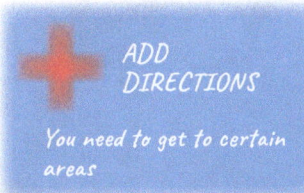

ADD DIRECTIONS

You need to get to certain areas

The activity is now 'multi-directional'.

JUST ONE DIRECTION

You have one goal or area to attack

The activity is now 'directional'.

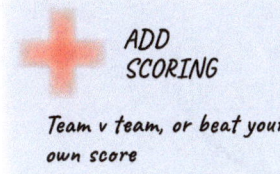

ADD SCORING

Team v team, or beat your own score

Increases competition and provides something to aim for and beat.

ADD CHOICE

One point if...
Two points if...

Increases collaboration; children manage their own level of challenge.

ADD CHALLENGE

Individual or team
Can you...?

A special challenge or support is provided or chosen.

ADDING MORE COMPLEXITY MAKES THE GAME MORE LIKE THE 'REAL THING'.

Using STEP to adjust the level of challenge

The examples below show how the STEP framework can be used by children and teachers to increase the level of challenge in a game. STEP can also be used to change games to offer support to children who need it.

STEP stands for:

Space   Task   Equipment   People

Space
Changing the space, size or shape of an area can have a big impact on the level of challenge that the game poses. For example, a dragon in Knights and Castles (page 71) could make their area bigger and this makes it harder to defend.

Task
Children don't always have to be doing the same thing as each other. They should be encouraged to make their task more difficult. One way of doing this is to use a scoring system where children get extra points for completing a more difficult task. In Flipper, for example (page 64), children could get double points for catching with their weaker hand.

T could also stand for Time. In Scarf Toss Challenge (page 65), for example, how many throws and catches can the children make in 30 seconds?

Equipment
Using different equipment is motivating for children. Try to allow them choice in what they use, and in how they use it. For example, in Floor Ball (page 70), a variety of striking objects could be provided, with thinner options like a rounders bat or a noodle being a more difficult option.

People
Adjusting the roles or numbers of people in a game is a good way of amending the level of challenge. In Cat and Mouse (page 67), a confident cat could play against two mice. In Floor Ball (page 70), you could play two players against one. Teams in games like Kho Kho (page 74) do not have to be of equal number – if you have two standout players, you could play them against a team of four or five others.

In Field of Dreams (page 144), allow children to choose which ball and striking object to use. This will encourage them to consider their own ability and confidence and to explore different challenges.

Capturing child voice and feedback in PE

Memories of school PE can last a lifetime and may affect future experiences of physical activity. Many adults have fond memories of PE, but others use words like embarrassing, humiliating or terrible to describe their experiences. As teachers, a minimum requirement of our role is that we 'do no harm'. No matter whether we think our lessons are fantastic or we know we are struggling and could improve, we would do well to ask the children what they think. Their feedback gives us the opportunity to critique our lessons, to identify any issues and to improve the children's experience.

Here are some ideas for how we might collect child feedback about PE simply and effectively, so we can understand their experiences, needs and feelings. November is a good time to do this, as it gives teachers time to digest the feedback and consider what adaptations may be necessary for the rest of the year.

A PE questionnaire

This could be a tick-box questionnaire or have emojis to circle. This could be ideal for KS1 children who may struggle to tell you in words how they are feeling.

How do you feel about your PE lessons this term?

Love them   Happy   Bored   Disappointed   Sad

Write a sentence or paragraph

This is a good chance to use classroom writing time to find out more about the children's feelings.

Complete the sentences.

- In PE, I like it when my teacher...

- One way I would improve PE is...

And/or: Write a paragraph describing your best PE experience, using at least four adjectives.

Class discussion or debate

This could be something you do in the last ten minutes of the day. You don't need to prepare a lot for it, but it could be really valuable.

Table discussion: What has been your best/worst PE lesson so far this term?

Class debate: One side of the room need to make an argument for doing less PE in school. The other need to make an argument for doing more PE in school. Hands up to talk and respond to each other.

Top TIPS for capturing child feedback

- Consider that the children's responses to your questions may depend on how you ask the questions and on their most recent experience, i.e. their last PE lesson. For example, if you ask them, 'Do you love PE?' straight after a brilliant lesson, then you may not capture a full range of experiences.

- Act on the feedback! Listen well and consider what PE is like for children in your class. Let the children know what you have heard and what actions you are going to take.

- Continue the dialogue. Check in a few weeks later to see whether your changes or actions have affected the children's experiences.

- A great PE curriculum is co-created by teachers, children and the community. Think of ways you could also get feedback from parents and families. Perhaps you could try a questionnaire for families asking them what they want from PE.

- Many schools work in networks or partnerships with other schools. There is value in having a network-wide review of PE and asking children from multiple schools the same questions about their PE experiences. This could be a great way to start sharing best practice.

Classroom design task

In pairs or threes, with a piece of flipchart paper for each group, children design their ideal PE lesson.

> On your flipchart paper, design your ideal PE lesson for your class. Think about everyone's needs and interests.
>
> Include: what the activity is, who is doing the activity, how everyone behaves, what help or input you want from your teacher, and anything else you think is important.

Focus group discussion

This might happen after some of the other methods, perhaps once you have identified who is not enjoying PE as much. It might be wise for these kinds of discussion to be hosted by another teacher the children know. This might make it easier for them to open up and speak honestly.

Keep numbers small, with a maximum of eight children, so they all get a chance to speak. Use open-ended questions. You could begin by asking questions like:

- How do you feel on a PE day?

- Tell me about your ideal PE lesson.

More information

- Ladwig, M. A., Vazou, S. and Ekkekakis, P. (2018), '"My best memory is when I was done with it": PE memories are associated with adult sedentary behavior', *Translational Journal of the American College of Sports Medicine*, 3, (16), 119–129.
- Brown, P. S. (2012), 'Introducing a negotiated curriculum', in: K. Irie and A. Stewart (eds.), *Realizing Autonomy*. London: Palgrave Macmillan.

Aim

To find imaginative ways to make a simple task more difficult.

Set-up

Grouping:
Individuals.

Equipment needed:
One beanbag per child.

Space needed:
Any.

Flipper

A throwing and catching coordination challenge for individuals.

How to facilitate the game

1 Explain the game. Spread some beanbags out, so children can easily get one each without a fuss. Challenge the children to place a beanbag on their foot, kick it up into the air and catch it with their hands.

2 Play. Most children will be able to do this, at least sometimes. Ask the children how they might make this task more difficult. If they really can't think of any ideas, you could offer a few alternatives such as catching it with their weaker hand, or even catching it on their head or with their other foot. But give them a chance first, perhaps in pairs, to come up with their own adaptations.

Adaptations

↑ This game can be progressed to a pair activity where the beanbags are kicked at the same time and swap places in the air. Can both partners catch each other's beanbags?

Assessment for learning

This task requires children to consider their own ability in relation to the difficulty of the task. They need to judge how much more difficult they can make the challenge and still ensure it is a realistic achievement. This will be difficult for some children, who might not be able to think of ways of making things harder or perhaps will think of things that are too difficult for them to achieve.

● How did you know if you needed to make the task more difficult?

● When you needed to make it more difficult, where did you get your ideas from?

Scarf toss challenge

A throwing and catching challenge for pairs.

How to facilitate the game

1 Demonstrate the game. Ask for a child to help you demonstrate. Give them a scarf and send them to stand facing you about three metres away. You each hold a scarf. On the count of three, you both throw your scarf directly up into the air. Then move quickly to swap places and catch each other's scarf before it drops to the floor.

2 Play. Children can find partners and scarfs and have a go. You may need to make sure pairs are not too close to each other in case of collisions while children look up at a scarf instead of around them. You could use lines, cones or spots on the floor to indicate starting positions in order to spread the children and pairs out and control the distance between them.

3 Adapt the activity. Pairs can move closer or further away from each other to make the challenge harder or easier.

Adaptations

For younger children, you could change this activity so there is just one scarf per pair. The pair start at one side of the area, and one of the pair throws the scarf ahead of them into the area. Their partner runs forward to catch the scarf, and then throws it ahead again for the other child to run to catch. In this way, they try to cross the area without the scarf dropping to the floor, using as few throws as possible.

Assessment for learning

There are at least two ways of measuring success in this game: pairs of children could consider how far apart they are when the scarf is thrown or they could count the number of successful throws and catches. Either of these methods is fine.

- How could you measure how well you did in this game?
- How did you and your partner challenge yourselves?
- What did you have to do well together in order to beat your score?

Aim

To work with a partner to measure and beat your score.

Set-up

Grouping:
Pairs.

Equipment needed:
One light scarf (or bib) per child. Optional: cones or spots.

Space needed:
Any.

Top TIP

This game also works well in larger groups. Children – each with a scarf – are arranged in a circle. They throw their scarf and then move clockwise to catch their neighbour's scarf. See Noodle Rush (page 193) for a similar game played with noodles.

With encouragement, children can find their own ways to challenge themselves. A mouse might decide to make the square smaller, to bounce a ball, or to run with one hand in their pocket.

Cat and mouse

A pairs chasing game around a shape on the floor.

How to facilitate the game

1 Demonstrate the game. Make a smallish square on the floor using four cones or markers. Choose a couple of volunteers to help you demonstrate. One will be the cat and one will be the mouse. The cat will chase the mouse around the outside of the square, trying to tag them. When the cat tags the mouse, the children switch roles.

2 Play. Once you have shown them the game, ask the children to find their own pairs or groups of three, get their own equipment and find their own space to set up and begin playing. It may be best for the children to be in a group of three, to allow them to switch roles and give each child a rest period while the others play (and so they can progress to one cat and two mice if appropriate).

3 Introduce levels. The cat chooses which level they want to start on. They should move up a level if they succeed.

● Level 1: Normal level – no restrictions.
● Level 2: Hold a ball in your hand.
● Level 3: Bend down to touch every cone you pass with your hand.

Adaptations

↑ Children can be encouraged to make up their own levels. Those above are just examples, but there may be many others that children could come up with themselves. See the STEP framework on page 61, which could be shown and taught to children as part of this activity. For example, you could ask the children to create a set of levels (this would be E for Equipment in the STEP framework).

Assessment for learning

Many children will be used to the concept of levels from playing video games. In this activity we want them to consider choosing levels that they find engaging and challenging. As their teacher, you will need to be comfortable that each pair or group of children may choose a different set of adjustments.

● What was the most challenging level you completed? What was hard about it?

● How did it feel when you got to a level that was too difficult (at first)?

 Aim
To create and use levels in order to manage and adjust the difficulty of the task.

 **Set-up**

Grouping:
Pairs or groups of three.

Equipment needed:
An assortment of objects to throw and catch (one ball per child would be perfect, but if not then children can take turns with what you have). Each pair or group also needs some cones or spots to make a shape on the floor.

Space needed:
Any.

Top TIP
Have a whiteboard with columns for Levels 1, 2 and 3. Children can come over and put their initials in when they complete a level. This provides a useful way of recording personal bests and measuring progress.

Aim

To work together to adjust an activity to make it more challenging.

Set-up

Grouping:
Pairs.

Equipment needed:
One ball per pair.

Space needed:
Any.

Shoot for the stars

A speed and accuracy challenge for pairs.

How to facilitate the game

1 Demonstrate the game. Choose someone to help you and send them to stand a few metres away. Ask them to do slow star jumps while facing away from you. Try to roll the ball so it rolls through their legs as they star jump.

2 Play. Tell the children to find a partner and a ball and have a go. After last month's work, they should know how to take turns already but this could be something you remind them of.

3 Measure success. There are a few ways that pairs of children could consider success. They could judge the distance between the roller and the jumper, or they could adjust the speed of the jumper or the number of consecutive successes. Ask the children to use their own measure of success and see if they can work together to beat their own scores.

Assessment for learning

This is a perfect activity for linking the social themes from September and October to this month's theme. The pair of children need to consider each other's needs and work together in order for the activity to be successful and to adjust the activity to make it more challenging.

- What did you change that made it more difficult? Was this the same for both of you?

- What skills did you need to improve in order to beat your own score?

Classroom debate

Who is mostly responsible for making sure you are challenged at school: you or your teacher(s)?

Double dribble

An individual challenge to dribble with two objects at the same time.

How to facilitate the game

1 Prepare. Get all the equipment spread out and easily accessible around the perimeter of the area.

2 Explain the game. Challenge the children to choose two different balls or objects and see if they can dribble them both at the same time. For example, can they dribble a football with their feet while also bouncing a basketball?

3 Play. Children can choose which balls or objects they start with and begin. You may need to revisit some of the work you did on sharing in September.

4 Observe and encourage. Share ideas between children and encourage each child to test themselves with something they find difficult.

Adaptations

For younger classes, the challenge could be modified to carry two different objects rather than dribble with them. So, for example, can they walk while carrying a ball in one hand and a beanbag on their head?

Assessment for learning

It can be hugely motivating to recognise our own improvement. Children can usefully learn the skills of reflecting on previous levels of performance and considering whether they have improved. This then leads to valuable discussions on how they have improved.

● Did you or any of your classmates improve or get better at this activity? How do you know they improved?

● What happens to your confidence when you can see that you have improved?

Aim
To demonstrate improvement or progress in self and others.

Set-up

Grouping:
Individuals.

Equipment needed:
Lots of balls in different shapes and sizes (at least two balls per child).

Space needed:
Any.

 Cross-curricular link

Think of two interesting adjectives, one to describe how you felt at the beginning of the activity and one to describe how you felt at the end of the activity.

Floor ball

A version of tennis, played by striking the ball along the floor.

Aim

To measure your own success and challenge yourself in a competitive game.

Set-up

Grouping:
Pairs.

Equipment needed:
One large, soft ball per court. One small, light bat or tennis racket (or other striking object) per child. Each court needs two tall cones to indicate the net.

Space needed:
You'll need a small court per pair.

How to facilitate the game

1 Demonstrate the game. Place two cones a couple of metres apart. Choose a child to help you demonstrate and give them a bat or racket. Work together to bat the ball back and forth along the floor between the cones. Each of you can only bat the ball once on your side of the cones.

2 Play. Tell the children to find a partner, set up their area and begin. Challenge them to see which pair can make the longest successful rally.

3 Add a scoring system. Change the aim of the game so it is now competitive. You score a point by batting the ball between the cones and past your opponent. Introduce a simple scoring system where the children play up to five points, with the first to get to five points being the winner.

Adaptations

For younger children, you could allow them to stop the ball by trapping it under their bat first, and then striking the stationary ball back.

Assessment for learning

Children may need help in how they measure their own success in a competitive game. The scoring system allows children to assess their progress beyond just winning and losing. For example, a child who wins 5-3 may now try to win by more points on their next attempt; a child who loses 5-0 may have an aim of scoring at least one point in their next game.

- If you won your game, how could you try to challenge yourself in the next game you play?

- If you lost your game, what would be a realistic challenge in your next game?

See page 56 for a photo of Floor Ball in action with a KS2 class.

Top **TIP**

If you don't have enough space, play doubles (two children per team), with players taking it in turns to strike the ball.

Knights and castles

A team game where points are scored by getting past the dragons.

How to facilitate the game

1 Tell a story. To begin with, young children may enjoy a brief story about some brave knights who are returning to defeat the scary dragons.

2 Demonstrate the game. Using four cones or markers make a square shape on the floor. Explain that this is a castle. Ask one child to hold a bib and go into the castle to be a dragon. Show the class how you – a brave knight – must try to get through the castle without the dragon catching you. The dragon can get the knight by tagging them with their hands.

3 Set up the area. You may have been able to set up the castles while the class were enjoying a quick starter game, but if not either add them now or give sets of four cones to the dragons and ask them to set up their own castles. For a class of 30, try six castles.

4 Play. Play the game once so everyone is clear on the rules.

5 Add teams and scoring. Put the children into teams of five or six each and add in the following scoring system:

- one point for getting through a castle
- two points for bouncing a ball through a castle
- three points for dribbling a ball with the feet.

Teams have a whiteboard each and collect their score on their whiteboard. Once they have gone through a castle, they need to come over to their team whiteboard to add their score. Play three or four games, changing the dragons each time.

Adaptations

↓ It may be easier to start this game as an individual game, with everyone keeping their own score. Then, once the children are ready, add in the team element and team score-keeping.

↑ A nice addition is to add some treasure to each castle – perhaps a few floor spots in the middle of each – which the knights must try to retrieve for extra points.

Assessment for learning

Some teams will score more points than others. The teacher's role is to help each team recognise their own personal best and challenge them to try to beat it. After they have had a couple of games, ask each team to reflect for a few minutes and come up with their own challenge for the next game. This could be a total score they want to try to achieve or a particular way of scoring points.

- What helped you to decide your own team challenge?
- What happened to your experience of the game once your team had decided on their team challenge?

Aim

To try to achieve a personal best as a team and to recognise the effect of a team challenge on motivation and engagement.

Set-up

Grouping:
Pairs and groups of five or six.

Equipment needed:
24 floor spots to denote six castles on the floor. A bib, a ball and a whiteboard per team.

Space needed:
This can work in a small space, as the castles can be small and close together.

It is easiest to show the children the playing area if you take them to the side of the area (rather than sitting them in the middle). A whiteboard is also a helpful tool.

71

Aim

To support each other to choose more difficult options.

Set-up

Grouping:
Groups of no more than eight.

Equipment needed:
Cones or spots to make a large square or rectangular area per group.

Space needed:
Four to six courts for a class of 30. Each area can be small.

Chicken, wizard, hero

A tag game in which you can be bold and go alone or be safe and stay with the pack.

How to facilitate the game

1 Show the area. Take the children to the outside of the area so they can see the perimeter and boundaries within which the game will happen. The game takes place in a large square or rectangle. You can mark this out with a cone or spot in each corner.

2 Show the game. Choose four to eight children to play. Choose one of them to go into the middle of the area and be the tagger. The other children (the runners) line up along one edge of the area. The task for the runners is to get to the other side without getting tagged. If they get tagged, they join the tagger in the middle.

3 Explain the rules. This is how the game works: the tagger in the middle chooses one of the runners and calls their name. The chosen child can choose one of the following:

● **Chicken –** if they call out 'Chicken!' then all the runners run at once.

● **Wizard –** if they call out 'Wizard!' then they can cast a spell on the taggers before running alone across the area. The spell might be something like: 'Taggers can only hop on one foot.' As soon as the wizard either gets tagged or reaches the other side safely, all the other runners try to run across without getting tagged.

● **Hero –** if they call out 'Hero!' then they run across on their own with no spell. As soon as they either get tagged or reach the other side safely, all the other runners try to run across without getting tagged.

4 Play. Ask groups of children to set up their own area using spots, choose a tagger and begin.

Adaptations

↓ Removing the wizard option makes the game quicker and simpler.

Assessment for learning

Chicken, Wizard, Hero allows the child whose name is called to adjust their level of challenge depending on how confident they feel. This is a good activity for helping children understand each other's experiences. More confident children may be excited to run alone against the taggers. Other children may not enjoy that experience and may be reluctant to choose the wizard or hero options. By understanding how others feel, the children will be better placed to support each other to do more challenging things.

● How did it feel when your name was called? How did other people feel when their name was called?

● Why is it sometimes worrying to have to do difficult things when all your friends are watching? How can your friends help you in this situation?

Super striker

A small-group striking and fielding game.

How to facilitate the game

1 Show the game. Place a ball on top of a tall cone. Ask three children to come out to be 'fielders'. Set up some targets to aim for (there should be at least one more target than there are fielders). Targets could be big, like mats, or small, like a small cone. Demonstrate hitting the ball off the cone with your hand (or a bat or racket) and aiming to hit one of the targets. The fielder should try to stop the ball from hitting the targets and retrieve the ball as quickly as possible.

2 Play. Ask groups of children to set up their areas and take it in turns to bat.

3 Introduce a scoring system. Give points for each target, so targets that are further away and/or smaller are worth more. Each batter has three strikes and adds up their total score. Switch the batters after three strikes so everyone takes turns to bat.

Assessment for learning

Let the children get used to the basic version of the game, so allow each child to have three bats each. After that, it is worth asking the following questions to get children considering how they can take further ownership of their own level of challenge.

- How might you adjust the scoring for different objects, bats and ways of serving? (Consider that for the most confident children, typically in older classes, the ball could be served to them by a fielder, either in the air to be batted or on the floor to be kicked.)

- How might the fielders score points?

- Does everyone need to have the same scoring system?

Top TIP

Use objects in your playground area or natural environment as targets. For example, a tree could be worth five points, or a climbing frame three points. You could also use tyres or footballs as interesting targets.

 ## Aim

To design a scoring system which challenges you to try harder tasks.

Set-up

Grouping:
Groups of three to five.

Equipment needed:
Each group will need some equipment to mark spots on the floor and set up targets to aim for. They will also need bats and rackets, and a tall cone to balance a ball on.

Space needed:
Several areas could be set up in a small space. (See page xvii for a diagram showing an example set-up.)

Aim

To try to achieve a personal best as an individual within a team game.

Set-up

Grouping:
Teams of four or five.

Equipment needed:
Each court needs lines to denote boundaries and a centre line, so floor spots may be needed for this.

Space needed:
Each court will host two teams playing against each other. Courts can be small.

Kho kho

A strategic team game of chasing, tagging and escaping for Key Stage 2.

How to facilitate the game

1 Show the area. The Kho Kho court is a rectangle that is split in half by a centre line running lengthways, so it looks like two long, thin rectangles next to each other.

2 Explain the game. Two teams of four or five players play against each other in this modified version of the game. One of the teams, the 'chasing' team, spreads out and kneels down along the centre line on the court. The other team is the 'running' team, and they start the game in one of the rectangles. One of the chasing team gets up to chase the runners and try to tag them. If they tag them, the child they tag must remain still until released with a high-five by a teammate. The chasing team needs to try to tag all the runners.

3 Explain the rules. The running team can cross the central line in order to get away from the chaser. But the chaser cannot cross the central line. Instead, the chaser can tag and replace one of their teammates on the central line, who can then get up to run into the other half of the court to chase the runners.

4 Play. The game could be played within a time limit, say 90 seconds, with the winning team being the one who can tag the most opposition players in that time.

Adaptations

This can be a fast-paced tag game full of quick decisions and engagement. But it may also be tricky for children to understand and enjoy. You will need to observe and assess which progressions or adjustments would add value without overcomplicating the basic game.

↓ You could make the task easier for the chasing team by allowing two players to chase at once. This would also mean that more players were involved at once.

↑ You could add a ball to the running team, which they need to throw and catch between them. If the ball is touched or intercepted by the tagger, then the teams switch places. Runners can still be frozen with a tag.

TopTIP

With a new game like this, it might be worth showing a YouTube video of the game in action before leaving the classroom for the PE lesson. This will help the children understand what the adult version of the game looks like.

In real Kho Kho, the players in the chasing team on the centre line face alternate directions and can only enter into the side of the court they are facing.

Assessment for learning

This might be a tricky game for some children to understand and succeed in, so success may look very different from one child to the next. Learning how the game works and following the rules may be enough of a challenge for some children to begin with.

● What was most difficult for you when we first started playing?

● How did your experience of the activity change as you got used to it?

● What did you achieve in this game? What did success look like for you?

Kho Kho   Three small courts for a class of 30

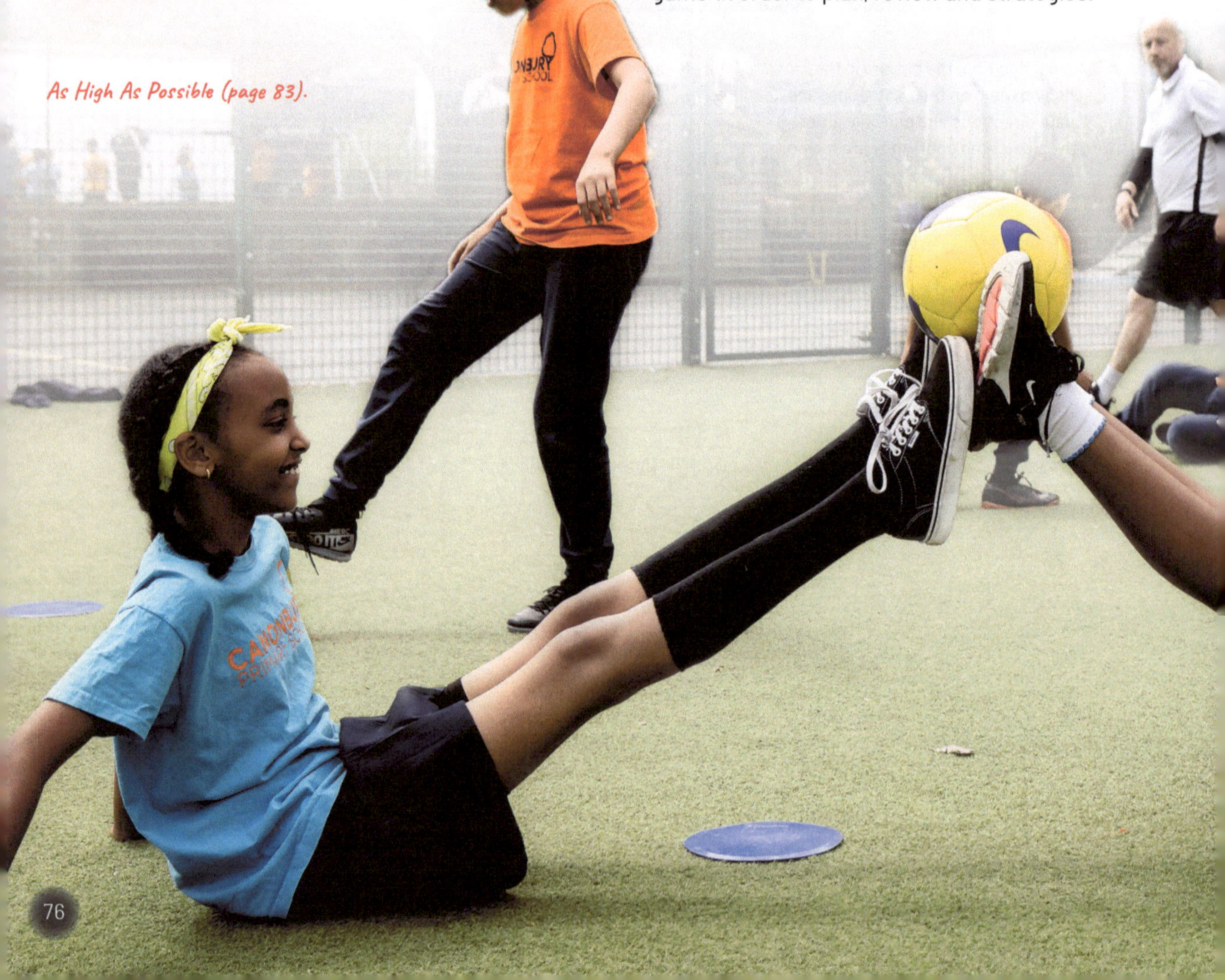

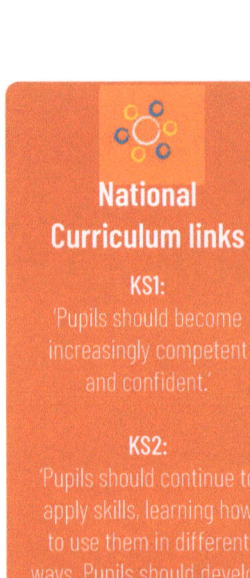

December

Problem-solving in games

National Curriculum links

KS1:
'Pupils should become increasingly competent and confident.'

KS2:
'Pupils should continue to apply skills, learning how to use them in different ways. Pupils should develop an understanding of how to improve in different physical activities.'

An introduction to problem-solving in games

PE offers the perfect opportunity to begin thinking about our thinking. In December, children will explore how they solve problems and examine what it means to be a 'good learner'. Games this month include individual, pair and team problem-solving, where children are encouraged to 'pause the game' in order to plan, review and strategise.

As High As Possible (page 83).

A child's confidence can be enhanced when they become more competent at seeking information, sharing ideas and trying new solutions. This month's theme provides important learning to help prepare the children for examining tactics and strategies, which are a focus of the KS3 National Curriculum in secondary school PE. Problem-solving skills can also be linked to other areas of the school curriculum.

This month, Netball Legends 2 (page 92) provides an example of how we can use a digital video games approach to engage children in planning and reviewing and in setting problems for others in games.

By this point in the school year, it has really started to get dark and cold outdoors, so activities in December and January have been chosen because they can work in a smaller indoor space. A varied selection of quick starters like As High As Possible (page 83), Bench Swap (page 85), Dice Balance (page 80) and Floor Is Lava (page 82) will all work really well to get everyone moving and learning in a small indoor hall. Advice on how to design and deliver high-quality PE in small spaces is given on page 78.

Key skills

- Seeking and gathering relevant information
- Defining the problem and making a plan
- Sharing and explaining ideas to each other
- Including everyone and actively listening to each other
- Being creative and trying new things
- Solving problems 'on the go'
- Setting problems for others
- Thinking about how we solve problems

Top tips for PE in small spaces

If you have to take your PE lessons indoors, or if you have limited outdoor space in your setting, try these top tips for designing and delivering high-engagement PE in small areas.

1 Teach children how to move in a crowded area. If you are worried about everyone moving in a small space then spend some time teaching the children the skills needed to move safely:

- **Look** before they move.
- **Move** with caution.
- **React** to the movements of others by keeping their heads and eyes up to continually scan around them.

2 Amend the game using the STEP framework (page 61). The games you use should be modified from the adult versions. An example is Sitting Volleyball (page 52), which has been amended to a reduced team and court size and a seated position. This allows many courts to be set up within the same small space.

3 Use small-group or pair games. As well as the quick starter games in this chapter, games like Scoop (page 175) or Arm Tennis (page 174) are great for small spaces because they offer lots of engaging movement repetitions within a confined space.

4 Be clever with lesson design. Consider 'wave' activities like in Secret Agent (page 202) where all the children move in the same direction. This set-up can include a safe channel for children to return along, which reduces the chance of collision. A carousel approach to lesson design is explored on page 97 and is perfect for offering variety within a small space.

5 Stay out of their way. Teachers and other adults should observe games from the side of the space. If space is limited, the children don't need you in the middle of the area. Find sensible spots at the side of the activity to observe and teach from.

6 Manage small-sided games carefully. You may not be able to get all the children moving in small-sided games in a small space. See ideas on page 190 for how to keep the engagement of children who are waiting their turn to play.

'One person who...': Problem-solving in team games

A framework for assigning problems or challenges to children in team games

The 'one person who...' framework allows the teacher to provide specific challenges to individuals within team games. This framework could offer additional and more complex problems to teams who have worked out the initial problem posed by the game or who need extra challenges in order to maintain engagement or even-up competitive contests against other teams. 'One person who...' also allows games to be extended beyond their initial version so problems can be explored over more than one lesson.

In order to use this framework, the teacher needs to spend time preparing a selection of conditions, constraints or challenges for individuals within the team game.

In Turn the Goal (page 90), goals that face in different directions pose new problems to solve.

Example

If playing Turn the Goal in teams of five (page 90), this might be the selection of conditions:

One person who....

1. ... is the only one on the team who is allowed to give instructions.

2. ... can use their hands anywhere on the pitch.

3. ... cannot pass the ball forwards, only sideways or backwards.

4. ... must quickly resolve any conflicts or arguments that arise during the game.

5. ... cannot speak at all.

The teacher could assign roles to each child within each team. Alternatively, teams could be shown the options and given time to assign someone to each role.

This idea could be progressed so children choose their own constraints or design their own 'one person who...' menu for their opponents.

This framework allows the teacher to use a 'numbered heads together' approach to aid learning. This works by asking all children with the same number to leave their team and get together to share experiences, ideas and understanding. (Also see cooperative learning on page 33.)

Aim
To try creative
solutions and steal
ideas from others.

Set-up

Grouping:
Pairs.

Equipment needed:
One mat and one dice
per pair.

Space needed:
Any space will work.

Dice balance

*Pairs of children roll a dice and complete
a gymnastics balance challenge.*

How to facilitate the game

1 Demonstrate the game. Ask the children to find a partner and a mat. Challenge them to make a balance together where one of the pair is supporting the other and they have four body parts between them touching the floor.

2 Add a dice per pair. Each pair will roll their dice. Whatever number shows on the dice, that is the number of body parts that can be touching the mat during the balance. Challenge children to hold their balance for ten seconds. If they roll the same number twice, they must think of a different balance pose than the first time.

3 Play. This activity can be made into a game by adding some competition, for example: who will be the first pair to create a supporting balance for all the numbers one to six?

Assessment for learning

This activity promotes problem-solving through action. It is not sufficient to describe a solution in words, but pairs of children will need to act out the solution physically to see if it works. Sometimes they may be stuck for ideas, and the following questions might help them reflect on their creative process.

- After you rolled the dice, what typically happened in order to get to a successful solution? (Think about the mixture of talking and moving, and focus on how sometimes you don't know the answer in words but can work it out physically with your body through movement.)

- When you got stuck, where did your new ideas come from?

Top TIP
If you don't have any or enough dice, just call out numbers instead. Alternatively, pairs of children could choose numbers for their neighbouring pairs to try.

Floor is lava

A whole-class movement challenge where players must avoid falling in the lava.

Aim

To explore what information you need in order to solve the problem.

Set-up

Grouping:
Whole class together.

Equipment needed:
Benches, mats and climbing apparatus to make volcanoes for children to climb onto; two floor spots per child.

Space needed:
A playground is ideal or you could use a similar indoor set-up.

How to facilitate the game

1 Set up the area. Children could help with this. You want a play area with a variety of obstacles and apparatus that provide safe places from the 'lava' (the floor).

2 Set the task. Children need to try to get from one obstacle or apparatus to another without stepping in the lava (touching the floor). They should use some objects to help them. For example, each child could have two floor spots each and might be able to explore the area by stepping onto and moving the spots.

3 Make it a challenge. Can the children visit all the different volcanoes (apparatus) without falling in the lava? They get a point for each volcano they can successfully get to.

Adaptations

↑ To increase the scale of the problem, children could be in pairs or teams of three, with a limited amount of equipment between them. They need to solve the problem of getting the team from one volcano to another.

Assessment for learning

This will probably be an activity that the children improve at over time, so much so that they will become quite competent at moving around the area after a while. It is worth reflecting on the process of trial and error that led to this success.

● What did you try which didn't work?

● What is the most important thing you need to know or do in order to get around the area without falling in the lava? (Focus on how you found a successful way of moving.)

 Cross-curricular link

Lava can reach temperatures of 1,000 degrees Celsius. However, unless it is on a steep slope, lava usually moves quite slowly, at about one mile per hour.

As high as possible

Pairs use trial and error to solve a movement problem.

How to facilitate the game

1 Explain the rules. Two children must get a ball as high off the floor as possible. But they need to follow three rules:

● The ball must start on the floor.

● Both people must be touching the ball for the whole time.

● You can't touch the ball with your hands or arms.

2 Play. 'Find a partner, find a ball and off you go.' The children don't need more information than that. Don't give them any more clues. They need to solve the problem themselves. Your role is to check they have understood and are following the rules.

Adaptations

↓ A soft, squidgy ball will be easier for children to grip than a hard ball.

↑ Pairs of children who are successful before others might need an additional challenge. This provides the opportunity to revisit last month's work on 'challenging yourself' and you could ask them to find ways of making the task harder so they remain challenged. If they need support with this, two ways of extending the task could be:

● Can you get the ball from floor to head height in less than ten seconds? Can you beat your own time?

● How many ways can you get the ball from floor to head height?

Assessment for learning

The highest possible height to get the ball is head height, and this can be achieved most easily by the pair working together to clamp the ball between their heads and lift it from the floor. But typically, children will start the activity using their feet, not their heads.

● What was the most difficult aspect of the problem to begin with?

● Where did you get new ideas from?

● How quickly did these ideas spread through the group?

See page 76 for a photo of the game in action with a KS2 class.

Aim

To define the problem and steal and develop ideas that other people are using.

Set-up

Grouping:
Pairs.

Equipment needed:
One ball per pair.

Space needed:
Any.

Top TIP

Write the rules on a whiteboard. That may help children to remember them and allow them to refer back to them.

Aim

To work together
to share and
develop tactics
and strategies.

Set-up

Grouping:
Groups of five to seven.

Equipment needed:
Spots or similar
to mark squares or
shapes on the ground.

Space needed:
Each group can make
their own small shape.

Cat in the corner

A game of quick decisions and movements for small groups.

How to facilitate the game

1 Demonstrate the game. Mark out a small square on the floor and ask one child to stand on each corner. Choose a fifth child to be the cat in the middle of the area. Ask the children in the corners to attempt to switch places with each other in any direction. They get a point each time they can successfully get to another corner. Only one child is allowed in a corner at any one time. The task for the cat is to get into a vacant corner while the others are switching places. If the cat achieves this, the child who is left without a corner becomes the new cat in the middle.

2 Play. Ask the class to get into groups of five, set up their areas and start the game. If you end up with some groups of six or seven, amend the shape to include more corners so all children are included and can play.

Adaptations

↑ The cat can tag a child who is between corners. This adaptation helps the cat. Making the shape bigger will also help the cat should you get someone stuck in the middle for a long time.

Assessment for learning

Once everyone has had a turn to be the cat, spend time sharing tactics that could be used to be successful in that role. Identify two or three key tactics and then play again.

● What is difficult about being the cat in the middle?

● When you are the cat, what can you do to give yourself the best chance of getting into a corner? (This could be done as a pair and share activity with key success criteria compiled on a whiteboard.)

 Cross-curricular link

You could play this game using a variety of shapes: triangle, square, pentagon, hexagon, heptagon or octagon, for example.

Bench swap

Two teams swap positions on benches without touching the floor.

How to facilitate the game

1 Set up the benches. You will need two benches in a V-shape, so they meet each other at the end.

2 Show the game. Select a group of ten children. Ask five children to go and stand on one bench and five on the other.

3 Set the challenge. The two teams of children need to swap places on the bench without anyone touching the floor. If someone touches the floor, they all need to start again from the beginning.

Adaptations

↑ Once the children have had a chance to work out a strategy, you could set this up as a race between different groups to see who can complete the task the fastest.

↑ To make this task more difficult, you could upturn one or both of the benches so the children have a much narrower standing area. Another option is to introduce a 'no touching each other' rule.

Assessment for learning

Most children will have ideas on how to solve this problem. The biggest challenge that this game presents is how ten children will communicate their ideas and cooperate and compromise with each other. Depending on how the children respond, one of the following questions could provide a useful reflection on how they tackled the problem collectively.

● What did you do when there were lots of different ideas in the group?

● Whose ideas were being heard and whose ideas were not being heard?

Aim

To share ideas as a group, listen to each other, and plan together.

Set-up

Grouping:
Groups of eight to ten.

Equipment needed:
Two benches per game (or you could use a line on the floor).

Space needed:
Any.

Aim

To solve problems
together within a
fast-moving game.

Set-up

Grouping:
Teams of three.

Equipment needed:
Each court will need
nine floor spots set out
in a three-by-three grid;
teams could wear
coloured bibs.
Optional: one ball
per team or child.

Space needed:
Each court hosts two
teams of three children,
competing against each
other. A class of 30
will need four courts,
with extra children
leading and refereeing
the games (rotate teams
so they all get to play
and lead). Spaces between
spots can be small so
multiple courts can fit
in a small space.

Three in a row

A quick-thinking competitive game where
children need to make a line of three to win.

How to facilitate the game

1 Set up one court. Use nine floor
spots to set out a three-by-three
grid on the floor.

2 Show the game. Two teams
of three (six children in total)
are asked to move round inside
the three-by-three grid. Assign a
seventh child to lead the activity.
The leader calls out a sequence of
instructions like '360 spin' or 'five star
jumps' or 'touch any two spots'. This
initial movement serves the purpose
of spreading the children out around
the area. When the leader shouts,
'Three in a row!', the game begins. On
this shout, the children need to move
quickly and the winning team is the
first to get their three players in a
row of three, joining any three spots
in a straight or diagonal line, and
putting their hands up and shouting,
'One!' You will need to make it clear
that only one child can occupy a spot
at any one time, and you may need
to add a rule that a child can only
be on a spot for a maximum of four
seconds before they need to move.

3 Play. Assign leaders to each
court and ask them to set up
their courts with floor spots. Send
two teams of three to each court.
Let the children explore the basic
game before you progress it.

4 Extend the rules. Later, once
everyone is used to the game
and rules, you can extend the game
so the winning team is the first to
get three rows of three (shouting
'1!', then '2!', then '3!' each time).
Importantly, the game does not
restart each time a line of three
is made, but the teams can move
from one line of three to another
as quickly as they are able.

Adaptations

The size of the grid will affect
the types of movement: a small,
compact grid will include lots of
starts and stops and changes in
direction, while a larger grid will
involve more sprints.

⬆ You could play a four-a-side game
on a four-by-four grid. You could
also add a ball per team or per child and
play the game with different ways of
moving or travelling with the ball. This
is a good game for using 'one person
who…' (page 79) in order to manage
difference and offer additional
challenges for older classes.

Assessment for learning

Children playing this game will need
to observe and respond to each
other's movements quickly. Children
will probably tell you that the key
to success in this game is good
communication, and this revelation
can broker useful discussions about
what good communication really is.

The green team solve the problem and get 'three-in-a-row'. Once the rules have been understood, the game should be sped up so teams need to make three different three-in-a-rows as quickly as they can.

● What kind of communication is most important in this game?

● How does it help to be able to see both your teammates the whole time? How might you move around the area to make this possible?

Cross-curricular link

How many different ways can you make three-in-a-row on a three-by-three grid? Answer: 8.

What about on a four-by-four grid? Answer: 24.

Three in a Row

Aim

To pause, change
or adapt the game
to make it more
difficult for
your partner.

Set-up

Grouping:
Pairs.

Equipment needed:
One tennis ball per child
and one tall cone per pair.

Space needed:
A wall.

Pro throw and move

*A competitive throwing and
catching pair game.*

How to facilitate the game

1 Demonstrate the game. Ask
for a child to join you. You should
each hold a tennis ball. Place a
cone in between you both, about
five metres from the wall. On a
countdown of 'Three, two, one,
throw!', both of you throw your ball
at the wall, and catch it on the
rebound. The first of you to then
touch the tall cone with your ball is
the winner. You get one point for
winning. Each player keeps their
own score.

*This simple game could become a
playtime favourite – if tennis balls
and cones are provided at breaktimes.*

2 Play. Let the children find a
partner and explore the game.

3 Add pauses. Each child can
pause the game whenever
they want. When they pause the
game, they are able to change the
game either to alter a rule or to add
some challenge for their partner.
For example, they could change the
scoring so they get two points if they
win using a throw and catch with no
bounce. There are also options to
amend the game by moving the cone
forward or back, or by introducing
'cheats' or 'superpowers'. Allow the
children to consider these options
in order to add new problems that
their partner has to solve.

Assessment for learning

Children may not want to pause the
game in mid-flow. But we want them
to see the 'pause the game' function
as a valid tool for reflecting on their
strategy and for re-planning.

- What does pausing the game allow
  you to do? What advantage does this
  give you?

- When you pause the game, you can set
  your partner a challenge. How did you
  decide what problem to give them?

Super Mario™ battle

A team game of pursuit and capture where problem-solving strategies are explored.

How to facilitate the game

1 Set up the area. It's a good idea to set up the area and equipment while the children are engaged in a quick starter game like As High As Possible (page 83). Get the jail areas arranged, and divide the children into three teams (using coloured bibs) while they are playing the quick starter game.

2 Explain the game. Super Mario™ Battle is a team game, where opposing teams need to locate and capture each other. It works well to have three teams, and the game is then played in the following way:

- Mario (red bibs) captures Luigi (green bibs).
- Luigi captures Princess Peach (yellow bibs).
- Princess Peach captures Mario.

To capture someone, you must kick or throw your ball so it hits their ball. When this happens, the person captured goes to jail. Jail could be a safe area where children can practise moving with the ball. They can be released when a teammate hits their ball. Alternatively, children could be rescued from jail by a high-five.

3 Play. Ask the children to spread out around the area, and count down – 'Three, two, one, play!' The winning team is the one that manages to jail all those they are pursuing first, or the one that has most others in their jail at the end of a set period of time.

Adaptations

↓ You could play this game without any balls and just as a tag game. So, players tag each other on the back in order to capture them.

↑ Each team has a different type of ball and a different way of moving with that ball, so the Reds could be a football team, the Yellows a hockey team and the Greens a basketball team.

Assessment for learning

This tag game is unusual because each child will have a team that is trying to capture them and a different team that they are trying to capture. This makes the game engaging and more complex than regular tag. The questions below aim to get children thinking about their own thinking.

- Is this tag game like other tag games you've played previously? What do you need to focus on in order to succeed?

- What do you need to do well in this game in order to avoid capture while helping your teammates?

Aim

To think about our own thinking during games.

Set-up

Grouping:
A whole-class tag game in three teams.

Equipment needed:
One ball per child; teams should wear coloured bibs.

Space needed:
This activity can work in a large or small space. Try to use some apparatus or obstacles for children to hide behind. Each team needs a 'jail' area, denoted by lines on the floor or a specific space.

Turn the goal

An invasion game where the goals are moved after a goal is scored.

Aim

To recognise changes
in the game and to
adjust strategies
accordingly.

Set-up

Grouping:
Teams of three to five.

Equipment needed:
One ball per game.
The children will need
to move the goals
in this game, so you
will also need two small,
lightweight football goals
or similar per game.

Space needed:
You'll need a large space
for this game to work well.
A netball court would be a
good size for one pitch.

How to facilitate the game

1 Set up a pitch. Show the boundary of the pitch you are using and put a lightweight football goal near each end. There should be space behind the goal so play can happen in that area (see the diagram below).

2 Show the game. Position two teams of three to five children each onto the pitch and ask one of them to choose which game to play: football, basketball, netball or handball. You could have hockey too if you have plastic hockey sticks. Whichever game they play, goals are scored in the football goal.

3 Turn the goal. Start the game, and when a goal is scored, the goalscorer runs over to the goal and moves it 90 degrees so it now faces sideways. Now that team has to score in a goal that faces in an odd direction, so they may need to adjust the way they attack to try to cope with this challenge. The next time they score, they move the goal 90 degrees again, and the goal is now facing away from them (you will need to have a bit of space behind the goal so it is still possible to score). The next goal scored moves the goal around 90 degrees again, and the fourth goal will bring it back to where it started.

Assessment for learning

Each time a goal is moved to face in a new direction, both teams need to change the way they defend or attack. This game is perfect for providing 'timeouts' for teams to discuss and adjust their tactics to respond to changes in the way the goals are facing.

● When was the goal easiest to attack or easiest to defend? Why?

● What do you need to do well as a team to respond to changes in the direction of the goals?

See photo on page 79.

Turn the Goal

Whoever scores a goal turns the goal 90 degrees

Top TIP

Before the lesson, discuss which sports have a timeout (e.g. basketball or futsal). Show the class a video of a basketball timeout on YouTube. Assign each team two timeouts during the game. This encourages them to make use of the opportunity to discuss tactics, as well as giving them the chance to problem-solve together.

A digital video games approach

Many children in primary school spend time playing video games and are familiar with the problem-solving processes and terminology that underpin engaging video game play. The video games approach to PE game design builds on this problem-solving experience, aiming to develop good learners, not just good players.

Why?

In a digital video games approach, children learn problem-solving skills such as: identifying relevant information, planning tactics, reviewing and setting problems for others. The games are engaging because they have high child ownership and minimal technical input from the teacher, and they contain a familiar video game vocabulary and format. The children decide when and how to intervene in the game, including the opportunity to set problems and challenges for their opponents. The overall goal is to help children to understand and control their own strategic thoughts while they are playing the game.

What?

Children explore a game with a mission to accomplish rather than a specific technical or tactical learning intention. Good game design involves careful planning and selection of five design principles taken from digital video games: a mission; level-ups; superpowers; pausing the game; and saving progress.

How?

You will need to design a game with a specific mission involving a problem to solve. You will need to consider how to make the mission more complex for successful teams, and how to adjust the game to make it easier or more difficult for individual children.

1. Explain the **mission** and **rules** to the children. Let the teams explore the game at the most basic level.

2. Introduce levels: A successful team can **move to the next level**. Each additional level poses more complex versions of the same problem. Children need to know what they must accomplish to move to the next level.

3. Introduce power-ups: When a player can demonstrate effective solutions to the problems in the game, they '**power up**', which changes the way they explore the game and offers them more difficult problems.

4. Introduce pausing: A player or team can **pause the game** in order to plan, review or make modifications. When they pause the game, they can choose to change the game in order to set a challenge for themselves or their opponents. (Children may not choose to use this function at first, so you may need to force a pause in the game to begin with.)

5. A team's progress can be **saved**. This means they can continue from the same level next time they play the game.

See Netball Legends 2 (page 92) for an example of the digital video games approach in action.

More information

- Gee, J. P. (2003), 'What video games have to teach us about learning and literacy', *Computers in Entertainment*, 1, (1).
- Gee, J. P. (2013), *Good Video Games and Learning* (2nd edn.). New York, NY: Peter Lang.
- Amy Price's website is full of resources and ideas: https://digitalgamesapproach.weebly.com

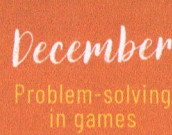

Aim

To observe the
game as it happens
and take in important
information about
your team and your
opponents' team.

Set-up

Grouping:
Teams of four or five.

Equipment needed:
Two balls per game.
Each team needs
five cones to defend.

Space needed:
Three small pitches are
needed for a class of 30.
(See diagram on
page xvii for the set-up.)

Netball legends 2

A Key Stage 2 invasion game with two balls
using a digital video games approach.

How to facilitate the game

1 Show the game. The game
is a netball game played on a
small court, using two balls instead
of one. Both balls are in play at the
same time. Each team has five
cones at their end of the court.
To score a point the ball must be
thrown or rolled so it hits a cone.
If a cone is hit, the point-scorer
steals the cone and takes it back
to their end of the court to add to
their collection of cones.

2 Introduce the mission. 'To
steal all the cones to win the
game.' Write this on a whiteboard
so it is clear.

3 Have a go! Let the children
explore the basic level of the
game. With two balls in play, they
will need to make lots of decisions
about whether to join the attack
or to defend.

4 Introduce levels. Teams move
up the levels depending on how
many cones they have at their end
of the court.

● Seven cones: They must pass before
they can score.

● Eight cones: They can only score
if they're more than two metres
from the cones. You might need
to insert a line with floor spots to
indicate this area.

● Nine cones: They need to be in
possession of both balls in order
to score a point and steal a cone.

5 Introduce superpowers.
If a player scores two points
in a row, they earn the power to
move three paces with the ball in
their hand.

6 Pause the game. Children
can pause the game to review
or plan tactics. They can also change
the game for themselves or their
opponents (to make it harder or
easier), for example:

● Challenge: They could nominate
which ball they need to score with
(but not tell their opponents).

● Cheat: They could move some of
their opponents' cones into the
middle of the court.

7 Save the game. Next time
you play the game, teams can
continue at the same level and
with the same superpowers
they accumulated.

Adaptations

This game could be played as a basketball, football, handball or hockey game instead.

Assessment for learning

Children playing this game will need to make lots of decisions about which ball to focus on, and how to be most useful to their team in defending or attacking.

● How does it help you if you observe your opponents as you play and identify what they do well and what they don't do so well?

● Did you manage to identify a problem you were having as you were playing? How might you solve this in the game?

A blue team player returns with a cone. The game continues to be played while she does this.

Top TIP

With this kind of complex game – with multiple progressions and lots to explore – it may be a good idea to play it over two or more lessons. This allows children to save their progress and gives them an opportunity to properly understand the challenges in the game so they can practise their problem-solving skills.

National Curriculum links

KS1:
'Pupils should be taught to master basic movements including throwing and catching and begin to apply these in a range of activities.'

KS2:
'Pupils should be taught to use throwing and catching in isolation and in combination.'

Key skills

- Being ready, reacting fast
- Throwing and catching with a racket or bat (striking)
- Throwing so that someone else can catch it
- Throwing for accuracy and/or distance
- Knowing when and why to use an underarm throw versus an overarm throw
- Catching: eyes on object; moving to adjust to the flight
- Throwing and catching in a variety of different game situations (application)
- Deciding when and where to throw and catch (decision-making)

January
Throwing and catching skills

An introduction to throwing and catching skills

Traditional PE lessons on throwing and catching typically focus on isolated technical practice (in pairs, for example) before moving into games for the last ten minutes of the lesson (five-a-side netball, for example). In this type of lesson, the gap between the isolated technical practice and the fully opposed game is vast, and techniques practised in the first part of the lesson bear little resemblance to the range of throwing and catching situations that children experience in the actual game.

Successful application of throwing and catching requires the children to know **how** to throw and catch (techniques) and also to make decisions based on **where**, **when** and **why** to throw and catch (skills). The underlying premise behind the games in this chapter is that throwing and catching techniques and skills can be learnt together within the context of modified games. Games like Cone Collector (page 106) and Noughts and Crosses (page 105) combine lots of repetitions of throwing in a motivating and challenging game which even young children can enjoy and succeed in.

Kudoda (page 104).

The key factor in learning throwing and catching may be the number of high-quality repetitions that each child experiences. Page 96 examines the concept of 'physically active learning time' and how we arrange and manage lessons which provide children with lots of chances to try, practise and improve. Teaching in PE may be best provided through the facilitation of reflection on success and by offering suggestions for improvement through carefully selected peer demonstrations.

Quick starters this month could be arranged in a carousel – this approach is described on page 97.

Physically active learning time

The KS1 and KS2 National Curriculum for PE requires teachers to 'ensure that all pupils are physically active for sustained periods of time'. It's important to consider the amount of physically active learning time children have in your PE lessons to make sure they get opportunities to explore movement and to 'learn by doing'.

On average, children in primary school PE lessons move for approximately one-third of a lesson (Fairclough and Stratton, 2006). A child learning to throw and catch may benefit from watching demonstrations, listening to advice and discussing progress with peers. However, a key factor that will determine successful progress is the number of high-quality repetitions of applied practice.

Physical learning time is the average amount of time in a lesson that each child has the opportunity to move and to learn by doing. It should not be seen as a measure of the success or quality of a lesson. However, if we believe that children need to practise physically in order to improve, then it may be important to consider how much physical learning time children get. There are also often strong links between inactivity and poor behaviour in PE.

Four top tips for increasing physically active learning time

1 Teach individuals. We know that all children are different, and they therefore need different levels of input from a teacher. In PE, the teacher should aim to work with individuals or small groups in the same way they do in a numeracy class. Try to resist stopping the whole group often, especially if what you plan to say is only relevant to some of the children.

2 Shorter interventions. Children won't listen for long, so make your interventions short and to the point. Before you intervene, plan what you are going to say or do. Sometimes a quick demonstration is better than two minutes of talking. Consider if you really need to bring all the children in from their game, or if you can freeze them quickly where they are, pose them a quick challenge, and then get them back to the game.

3 No queues. Relay races and line drills are not 'teamwork'. Queuing wastes learning time. A child in a queue of five children for 20 minutes has four minutes of learning time and 16 minutes of waiting time. Children waiting in lines are often bored and risk misbehaving because of this. Children need lots of repetitions in order to learn, and they need lots of engagement in order to behave well and enjoy their lesson.

Everyone can dribble a basketball at once – they don't need to take it in turns. Your lessons may look messier, but enjoyment, engagement and progress may be much better. Where you do need to use queues, aim to increase the number of stations or lines so the queues are shorter.

4 You can never be 'out'. Games like dodgeball often have a rule where children are 'out' – for example, when they are hit with a ball. Because of this, some children spend most of these activities sitting and watching rather than playing, moving and learning. If you use a game where children are 'out', find a way of getting them back in again quickly. For example, if they throw two beanbags into a hoop they can re-enter the game.

More information

- Fairclough, S. and Stratton, G. (2006), 'A review of physical activity levels during elementary school physical education', *Journal of Teaching in PE*, 25, 240–258.

Carousel lessons

A carousel lesson is one where children move around a set of games. This is useful for adding variety and challenge. This typically happens in gymnastics lessons where groups of about six or seven children work at a station for ten minutes, then move round to the next one. The same idea can be very easily applied to games too. At KS1, try a carousel of pair games, and at KS2 try a carousel of different small-sided games.

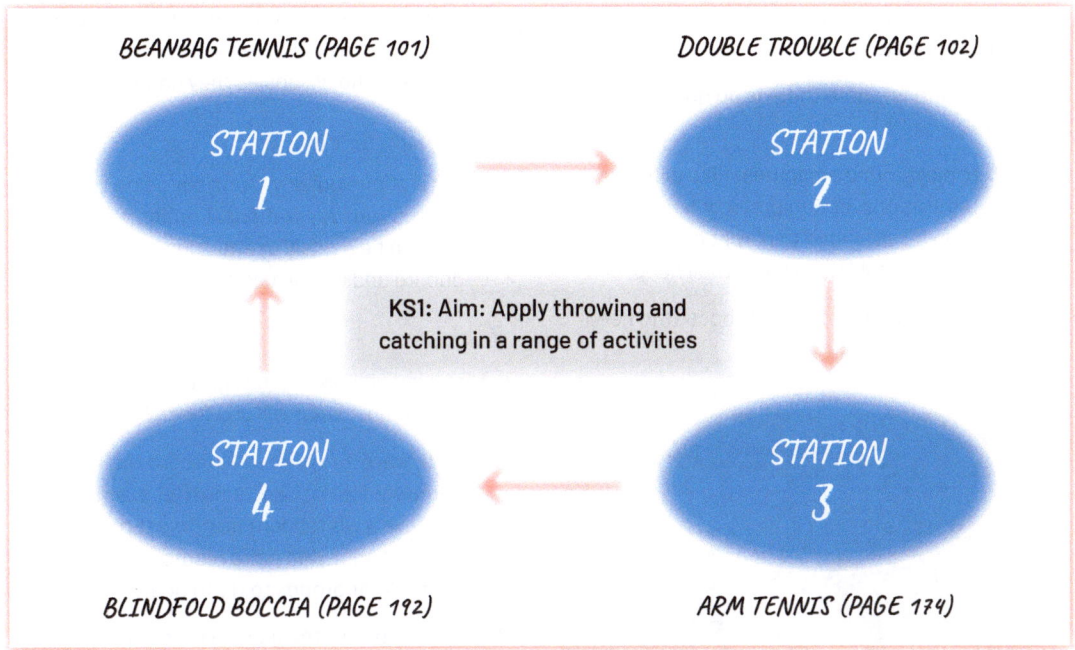

BEANBAG TENNIS (PAGE 101)   DOUBLE TROUBLE (PAGE 102)

STATION 1   STATION 2

KS1: Aim: Apply throwing and catching in a range of activities

STATION 4   STATION 3

BLINDFOLD BOCCIA (PAGE 192)   ARM TENNIS (PAGE 174)

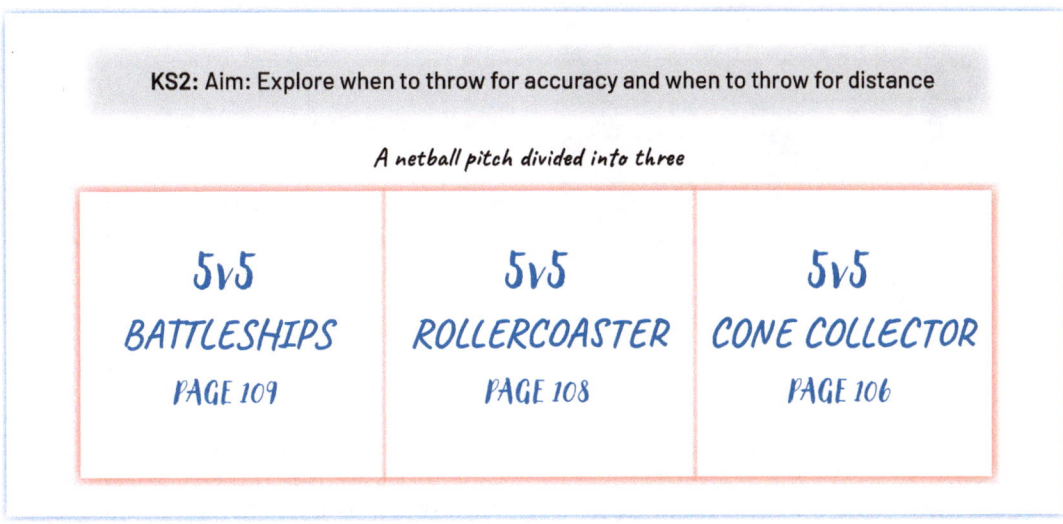

KS2: Aim: Explore when to throw for accuracy and when to throw for distance

A netball pitch divided into three

| 5v5 BATTLESHIPS PAGE 109 | 5v5 ROLLERCOASTER PAGE 108 | 5v5 CONE COLLECTOR PAGE 106 |

Top tips for delivering carousel PE lessons

Planning

- Choose stations that relate to your National Curriculum outcome.

- Choose stations that are simple, so they are easy to explain. You can always progress or add complexity later once children understand the basic activity.

- Choose stations where there is no queuing or waiting.

- Use fixed playground equipment (like climbing frames) as stations, or equipment where there isn't enough for everyone to play at once, such as a table tennis table or a basketball hoop.

- Plan how to extend stations for those who need a challenge.

Before the lesson

- Set up stations before children arrive if possible. Or ask the children to help with the set-up when they arrive.

- Work with teaching assistants (TAs) so they know how to help. For new or difficult stations, a TA could be asked to remain on that station and help all the groups as they come through.

Starting lessons

- Show stations quickly. Consider using labels or instructions for stations. Laminated station labels can be a really useful addition to the PE cupboard and can be used across the school.

Teaching

- Teach individuals or small groups. Plan interventions: what will you teach?

- Include ways for children to record their scores or compete for the best score (for example, you could have a whiteboard next to a throwing and catching station and pairs record their best rally score for later groups to try to beat).

- A quick pause of the game allows some groups to demonstrate their work, and this helps share ideas around the class.

Review and reflect

- Reflect on what worked and ask children what they think.

- For the next lesson: keep some stations, change some stations and replace some stations – based on your reflection on what worked well.

A carousel of four activities: Beanbag Tennis (page 101); Slam (page 137) with two hoops each; Four Square Pairs (page 160); Ring of Fire (page 118).

Five teaching styles for child ownership in PE

There is no single best way to teach PE. How you teach will depend on your confidence, your school and context, your children and what you want to achieve. Teachers may need to trial different styles of teaching and adapt and amend the style depending on how things go.

It can be tempting when teaching techniques like throwing and catching to use a very instructional style of teaching. Throwing and catching lessons in primary PE often involve teachers demonstrating a technique at the start of the lesson, with the children then practising that technique in isolation of any related game context for the remainder of the class.

As well as assuming that there is one true 'correct' technique that will suit everyone (which is often not the case), this approach provides little opportunity for trial and error or exploration. As we point out in the introduction (page xii), we can help include and engage all children by taking a more democratic approach to PE and by seeing our role as that of a facilitator rather than a commander.

Below are five different teaching styles taken from the spectrum of 11 styles developed by Mosston and Ashworth (2002). This section of their spectrum has been chosen as each style offers realistic opportunities for the children to choose, explore and solve problems for themselves while also ensuring a focus on specific National Curriculum content.

Inclusion style

- The teacher plans some games, including the various roles the children may take within each game.
- The children choose which game and role they feel best suits their interest and abilities.
- The teacher is a facilitator of the game.

Guided discovery style

- The teacher chooses a learning goal or aim and plans games related to that aim.
- The children explore the games.
- The teacher uses a series of questions to gradually help the children towards the learning aim.

Convergent discovery style

- The teacher selects a specific problem and plans games to explore this problem.
- The children play the games and try to find a possible solution.
- The teacher guides the children towards an appropriate answer.

Divergent discovery style

- The teacher selects specific problems and plans games to explore these problems.
- The children play the games and try to create different solutions.
- The teacher provides feedback on the creative process.

Learner-designed style

- The teacher chooses an area to focus on.
- The children design or adapt their own games in order to explore the focus area.
- The teacher is available to advise the children when asked to do so.

More information
- Mosston, M. and Ashworth, S. (2002), *Teaching Physical Education*. Pearson Education.

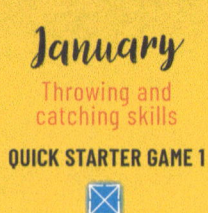

◎ Aim

To be ready and to react quickly.

Set-up

Grouping:
Pairs.

Equipment needed:
Two tennis balls per pair.

Space needed:
Any.

Quicksaver

Children must react fast to save the ball from reaching the floor.

How to facilitate the game

1 Demonstrate the game. Ask for a volunteer and give them two tennis balls, one to hold in each hand. Tell them to stand up and hold their arms outstretched away from them (so they make a T shape). Kneel in front of them. They will drop one of the tennis balls, and you need to try to grab it before it hits the floor (for three points) or before it bounces twice (for one point).

2 Play. Ask the children to find a partner and play. They have five turns each and then swap over. They should count their score.

Adaptations

↓ Scarfs or balloons will fall more slowly and are easier to catch.

↑ You can progress this game by having both balls dropped, one after the other. The catcher needs to grab both balls as soon as possible, with the same scoring system. The catcher could be challenged in various ways, for example, by starting further away or facing the other direction.

Assessment for learning

Our teaching must focus on the catcher. Our questions and discussion should aim to help them reflect on how they prepare their body and mind to react quickly.

● Where do you look and what do you focus on to help you react quickly?

● What do you need to do with your body to help you react quickly to the falling ball?

Top TIP

For younger children, add a hook or a theme to this game to make it relevant and engaging. For example, the balls could be meteorites falling to Earth, and they are the superhero who is the only one who can save the planet.

Beanbag tennis

A collaborative pairs game introducing racket skills.

How to facilitate the game

1 Demonstrate the game. A pair of children have a racket each. One of the pair places a beanbag onto their racket and tries to toss it to their partner so that their partner can catch the beanbag on their racket.

2 Play. Ask the children to find a partner and have a go. How many can they do in a row without dropping the beanbag?

Adaptations

↑ For older classes, add in a hoop between the two children. One of the children spins the hoop, and they then see how many successful passes of the beanbag they can make before the hoop falls.

↑ The main adjustment to this activity is to change the equipment. A beanbag is used as it does not bounce on the racket face and may provide quick success. For children who need more challenge, you could replace the beanbag with something bouncier like a tennis ball.

Assessment for learning

Racket skills can be tricky for many children and this activity helps to get them used to holding and manipulating a racket. For many children, the key success criteria for catching the beanbag will be to hold the racket so the face is flat and provides a large area for the beanbag to land. The exact questions you ask may depend on the level of the children, so it may be best to hold different conversations with different pairs, depending on their ability and success.

● How far apart should you stand from your partner?

● How could you hold the racket so it is easy to catch the beanbag?

● When might you need to move your feet forward, backwards or to the side?

Aim
To use a racket to pass and catch an object.

Set-up

Grouping:
Pairs.

Equipment needed:
One tennis racket per child. One beanbag and one hoop per pair.

Space needed:
Any.

Aim
To throw and catch with a partner.

Set-up

Grouping:
Pairs.

Equipment needed:
Two balls per pair (or other objects that can be thrown and caught, like beanbags, hoops or bibs).

Space needed:
Any.

Double trouble

A pairs throwing and catching challenge.

How to facilitate the game

1 Demonstrate the game. A pair of children stand facing each other, each with a ball in their hand. They must both throw the ball to each other at the same time so the balls cross in the air and both balls are caught.

2 Play. Children can find their own partner, their own equipment and their own space.

Adaptations

↑ A variety of equipment could be used. A more difficult version is for one child to have a ball and another a hoop. Both objects are thrown and the ball needs to move through the hoop in mid-air before both objects are caught.

↑ You could make this a game for threes, not pairs, and this increases the complexity. In this version, all three balls need to be thrown and caught simultaneously.

↑ You can increase the space between pairs to make this game more difficult.

Throwing and catching a ball is different to throwing and catching a hoop. Using a variety of equipment helps to challenge the children in new ways.

↑ Another option is to have one ball on the floor which is passed with the feet and one in the air which is passed with the hands (or maybe one chest pass and one bounce pass).

Assessment for learning

To be successful at this game, the children will need to work together to establish some kind of signal or command so they both throw at the same time. They will also need to work out how they coordinate their throws so the balls don't collide in the air. And, of course, they will need to practise a variety of throws and catches to be successful.

● What kinds of throws are easiest to catch?

● What do you need to do differently to catch a ball which arrives at waist height? What about a ball which arrives at head height?

● In what sports might you need and use the skills we have practised in this game?

Top TIP

Use the 'two stars and a wish' method (see page 189) to help pairs of children give feedback to each other.

Fireworks

Throwing and catching skills are tested in a fun individual challenge.

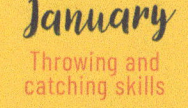

How to facilitate the game

1 Demonstrate the game. Take a tennis ball and put a scarf on top of it. Use an underarm throw to send the ball up into the air, so it takes the scarf up with it. As it reaches maximum height, the ball should fall more quickly, leaving the scarf falling more slowly. Catch the scarf as it comes down.

2 Play. Ask the children to have a go. Challenge them to see how many times they can successfully catch the scarf as it drops.

Adaptations

↑ The children catch both the ball first and then the scarf second without either hitting the ground.

↑ They could try catching the scarf with other body parts, not their hands.

↑ The children jump up and catch the scarf as early as they can.

Assessment for learning

This task focuses on both throwing and catching. Some children may find it difficult to throw the ball so it rises and falls above them. Others may not be able to track the flight of the falling scarf.

● Where and how do you need to throw the ball so you can easily catch the scarf?

● Why is the scarf easier to catch than the ball?

Place the scarf on top of the ball, then throw the ball underarm up into the air.

Aim
To throw directly up and to catch a slow-falling object.

Set-up

Grouping:
Individuals.

Equipment needed:
One tennis ball and one scarf each.

Space needed:
Any.

Top TIP

This is a good activity to talk about overarm and underarm throws. You could ask, 'Why is it better to use an underarm throw in this game? When might we want to use an overarm throw?'

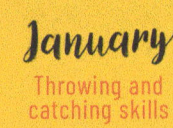

Aim

To throw objects so they are easy to catch and to be quick with your hands.

Set-up

Grouping:
Pairs or groups of three.

Equipment needed:
Each pair or group will need a large bowl or hoop plus a collection of about 12 to 15 small objects like dice or tennis balls.

Space needed:
Any.

Kudoda

A quick throwing and catching game from Zimbabwe.

How to facilitate the game

1 Demonstrate the game. Place all the dice (or tennis balls) into the bowl (or hoop). Sit or kneel next to the bowl in pairs or groups of three. Take one of the dice in your hand. Throw it into the air. While it is in the air, try to grab one or more dice from the bowl before catching the falling dice. If you succeed then you get to keep the dice that you grabbed from the bowl. It is now the next child's turn. The child with the most dice at the end is the winner.

2 Play. Ask the children to find a partner or a group of three and play.

Adaptations

↓ Try to experiment with different equipment. You can make it easier by using a lighter object – like a scarf – for the throwing and catching.

↑ This game can be made more difficult by asking the children to use one hand only. In this version, they need to throw, grab and catch all with the same hand.

↑ You could add in one dice or ball that is a different colour or shape. If a child picks up that one, they lose the game.

Assessment for learning

This game tests the children's coordination skills. It also tests their ability to throw accurately, in a way that allows them to catch easily. You can share ideas on tactics using the following questions.

● What are the advantages and disadvantages of throwing high into the air?

● What kinds of throws have been most successful?

See page 94 for a photo of this game in action with a KS2 class.

Cross-curricular link

Zimbabwe is a landlocked country. This means none of its border meets the sea. It is surrounded on all sides by other countries. Can you think of another country that is landlocked?

Noughts and crosses

A throwing and catching contest based on the popular noughts and crosses board game.

How to facilitate the game

1 Demonstrate the game.
Arrange the hoops in a three-by-three grid. Select a throwing line away from the grid. You could mark this with a cone or line. Teams take it in turns to throw and catch:

- One of the team takes a ball (or beanbag) and stands at the throwing line.

- A teammate goes to stand in one of the hoops.

- The thrower throws the ball and if the catcher catches it successfully, they leave the ball in the hoop.

- If the throw is not caught successfully, the team cannot leave the ball in the hoop.

The aim of the game is to make a successful line of three balls. The first team to do this wins.

2 Play. Ask the children to find a partner or a group of three and play against another team.

Adaptations

↓ For an easier object to catch, try tying a bib in a knot.

↑ To begin with, the rule is that you cannot 'steal' a hoop from the other team. In other words, if there is a ball in the hoop, you cannot stand and try to catch in that hoop. However, you could amend this rule so that hoops can be stolen.

↑ To add drama to the game, you could challenge teams to throw and catch in different ways. For example, if a team is throwing into their final hoop to make a row of three and win the game, then the throw needs to be made overhead (facing the other way) or between the legs.

↑ To increase the challenge, you could spread the hoops out to make the throwing distances longer.

Assessment for learning

This game challenges pairs of children to throw and catch successfully under the pressure of a competitive game.

- What kinds of throws are easiest to catch?

- Are you better at throwing or catching? What makes you think that? How might you improve in your weaker area?

Aim
To throw accurately over a variety of distances; to catch under pressure.

Cross-curricular link

- Noughts and crosses was first played by Ancient Egyptians around 1300 BC and was also a popular game in the Roman Empire.
- There are over 250,000 different outcomes of a game of noughts and crosses.

Set-up

Grouping:
Pairs or teams of three.

Equipment needed:
Each game will need nine hoops and five balls or beanbags in one colour and five balls or beanbags in a contrasting colour. Optional: one cone or line to mark the throwing line.

Space needed:
Any.

Rollercoaster

A competitive team game that develops rolling and fielding skills.

Aim

To roll the ball accurately and effectively and to collect a rolling ball.

Set-up

Grouping:
Teams of four or five.

Equipment needed:
Each game will need a small ball and goals to score in (you could use skittles to knock down if you don't have goals).

Space needed:
Each game is played on a small court. However, a larger space (or smaller teams) will make it easier to successfully roll the ball to each other. (See the diagram on page xvii for an example set-up.)

How to facilitate the game

1 Explain the game. The game involves two teams playing against each other, both trying to score by sending the ball into the opponents' goal. Players cannot run or move with the ball, and they must pass the ball by rolling it along the ground to a teammate.

2 Demonstrate a roll. To make it really clear how it works, ask for a volunteer. Show the class how to roll the ball along the floor to each other.

3 Play. Teams of children can begin games.

4 Demonstrate collecting a rolling ball. You may need to give children some help in how to effectively collect a ball that is rolling on the floor. They will need to move to 'get in line' with the ball so the ball arrives directly to them.

They will need to stoop down to collect the ball into their palms, stretching downwards, fingers first.

Assessment for learning

Throwing and catching skills include sending and receiving an object in many different ways. In this game, we explore how to send a ball by rolling and how to receive a ball which is rolling. These techniques may be used when fielding in striking and fielding games like cricket.

- What do you need to do well in order to roll the ball quickly and accurately? (Answer: bend low, roll with one hand, release the ball at ground level and follow through with your arm.)

- What do you need to do well in order to collect a ball which is rolling near you? (Answer: get in line with the ball so your feet are in the way of the ball and bend low to scoop the ball up with your hands.)

Top TIPS

If you play invasion games and you find they are slow and lack intensity, try adding a second ball into the game. Having two balls in play instead of one means twice as many repetitions of ball techniques per child.

To deal with unequal teams, you could use:
- scoring systems that include everyone (page 40)
- the STEP framework (page 61)
- one person who... (page 79)

Battleships

A throwing and catching contest based on the popular battleships game.

How to facilitate the game

1 Show the area. The game takes place on a small rectangular court with a centre line in the middle. Each team sets up five battleships in their half of the court. Each battleship could be a tall cone, a hoop, a floor spot or similar. Teams need to agree on what battleships they are using and both should set up the same number and type of battleships. The aim of the game is to sink all of the opponents' battleships. The first team to do this wins the game.

2 Demonstrate the game. To sink a battleship, you take a missile (a beanbag or other object) and throw it from your half of the court, aiming to hit one of the opponents' battleships. If you hit a battleship, that battleship is removed from the court. To begin with, teams take it in turns to throw. If you are indoors on a smooth surface, you could also allow them to slide the missile along the floor (instead of throwing it).

3 Play. Ask the children to find a group of three or four, get their equipment and set up ready to play.

Adaptations

↑ To speed up the game, teams don't need to take it in turns. Instead they can throw whenever they want. This works if you give each team four missiles to start with.

↑ You could also allow players to guard or defend their battleships and stop the missiles from hitting them. They might do this by trying to catch the missile as it is in mid-air, for example.

Assessment for learning

This game challenges children to throw (or send) an object accurately. They may need to experiment with different types of throwing or sending in order to find what works best for them.

● When might you use an overarm throw and when might you use an underarm throw? Why?

● Are there other ways of firing your missile which are even better?

Aim

To throw accurately over a variety of distances.

Set-up

Grouping:
Teams of three or four.

Equipment needed:
Each game will need a variety of tall cones, hoops and targets, plus a selection of throwing objects (e.g. tennis balls, beanbags).

Space needed:
Each game will be played between two teams on a small rectangular court. (See diagram on page xvii for an example set-up.)

Top TIP

This game could be made more accessible if children throw from a seated position. If you provide each court with a chair, then wheelchair users can play at the same level as their classmates.

Top·**TIP**

The game should involve lots
of repetitions of throwing
and catching per child.
The teacher needs to make
sure that all children are
included and that the game
is not dominated by one or
two players on each team
at the expense of others.
To aid inclusion, see ideas
like the Autograph game on
page 40.

Newcombe

A traditional team throwing and catching game for Key Stage 2.

How to facilitate the game

1 Show the court. The game takes place between two teams, with one team on either side of a high net or rope that runs along the centre of the court.

2 Demonstrate the game. The game consists of throwing the ball over the net, aiming for the ball to touch the ground on the opponents' side of the court. If the ball hits the floor on the opponents' side of the net, then you score a point. The opponents try to intercept the ball by catching it and then throw it back over the net. Children may not run with or kick the ball and must throw or pass from the point at which it was caught.

3 Play. Ask the children to get into teams of four or five and start a game.

Adaptations

If you find the game is slow and lacks intensity, you can try renaming the game 'Hot Potato' and adding in the following rule: each player can only hold the ball for three seconds. If they hold it for longer then it burns them and the opponents score a point. If you really want to add to the intensity (for very able players on small courts), you could introduce a second ball to the game and play with two balls instead of one.

Assessment for learning

This game was recommended for primary schools in the 1933 edition of *Physical Training for Schools*, a national PE manual for class teachers. It is a version of volleyball but without the volleying. The questions you ask will depend on the level of skill displayed by the children and whether you need to focus on techniques or tactics.

Techniques:

● What helps you to catch a falling ball? (Answer: eyes on the ball, body and hands ready.)

● What kinds of throw might be best to get the ball up and over the net? (Answer: probably an underarm throw will send the ball up best.)

Tactics:

● How might you make the opponents move so there is space to score a point? (Answer: you could pretend to throw in one direction and then change at the last second.)

● When and why might you decide to pass the ball to a teammate first instead of throwing it back over the net? (Answer: if they are in a better position to return the ball over the net.)

Aim

To throw a high ball and to catch a falling ball.

Set-up

Grouping:
Teams of four or five.

Equipment needed:
Each game will need a volleyball (or similar). Each game is played on a court with a net or rope stretching across the ground a little over the height of the children's reach. You could put a line of cones close to the net to indicate a no-go zone to keep the children away from the net.

Space needed:
Three small courts work well for a class of 30.

111

National Curriculum links

KS1:
'Pupils should be taught to master basic movements including running and jumping and begin to apply these in a range of activities.'

KS2:
'Pupils should be taught to use running and jumping in isolation and in combination.'

Key skills

- Being ready to move (physically and mentally)
- Practising fast acceleration and deceleration (being low to the floor)
- Changing speed and direction to get past defenders
- Using a variety of jumps and landings, including hopping
- Jumping for distance and accuracy (jumping through, in, over, around)
- Timing of jumps to clear moving obstacles
- Landing softly, and being ready to go again (soft, quiet landings)
- Deciding when and where to run and jump (decision-making)

February

Running and jumping skills

An introduction to running and jumping skills

Running and jumping are key movements in so much physical activity and in so many different sports. In this chapter, we consider what we really mean by running and jumping skills, and how we might deliver and teach age-appropriate games that help children understand and apply them.

Importantly, we need to consider that the terms 'running' and 'jumping' describe a huge variety of actions and movements. For example, jumping could be from one foot to another, with both feet together, or hopping on one foot. You could jump for distance or for accuracy. You could jump to catch or reach something. You could jump over something, onto something, off something or around something. You could jump to avoid something or to get something. You could jump from a stationary position, you could jump while running, or you could jump up from the ground.

Running is also more complex than it might seem. To be able to run in a straight line at speed is just part of the repertoire needed to move well in games. In fact, within the context of games, it is rare for running to take place at speed with nothing but space to move into. In reality, movements take place in contexts which are continually changing.

This month, games like Robin Hood (page 121) and The Great Fire of London (page 128) mix running and jumping skills together and challenge children to use these skills in real-game contexts. Quick starters like Noodle Skipping (page 116) and Hoop Jump (page 120) are perfect for developing movements in young children.

Noodle Skipping (page 116).

Five top tips for giving feedback in PE

In primary PE, feedback typically only occurs at the end of the lesson, and usually to the whole class at once. Teachers need to consider the specific, individual feedback they provide to children in numeracy and literacy lessons and try to find ways of recreating similar processes in PE.

1 Feedback should be linked to the learning intentions

Feedback to children should aim to help them understand one or more of the three elements in the diagram. If children know and understand: (1) where they are now; (2) what they are trying to achieve; and (3) how to get there, then there is a really strong chance they will make progress.

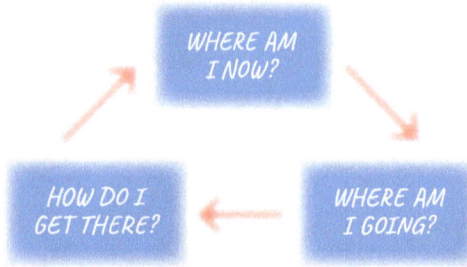

WHERE AM I NOW?

WHERE AM I GOING?

HOW DO I GET THERE?

2 Feedback should be specific to the individual child

Each child has specific needs and feedback should acknowledge this. Base your feedback on observations you make. Effective and impactful feedback in PE might be best delivered one-on-one by taking a child to the side of the activity to discuss their progress. Working with pairs or small groups might also work well.

3 Feedback during the learning, not after the learning

Don't leave feedback until the end of the lesson or the end of the topic or month. Children need to get early feedback so there is still time for them to digest it, understand it and act on it.

4 Feedback needn't take long

Sometimes, children may need to spend five to ten minutes of a lesson considering how they are doing. At other times, when it's cold outside, for example, you may want to maintain higher physically active learning time. Consider 'drive-by' feedback, where you might give some quick, verbal feedback to a specific child or group as you walk past their game.

5 Feedback doesn't have to be about techniques or sport performance

Feedback in PE needn't be sport-specific or in the language of a coach. Of course, it is helpful for children to understand how they can improve technically. However, it may be just as (or more) important that they receive feedback on their behaviour, effort or collaborative skills.

Feedback is often most effective when provided to individuals or small groups (rather than the whole class at once). This allows the feedback to be specific to the progress each group is making.

Create your own whole-class tag game

Whether you call it tag, tig or it, these kinds of chasing games are hugely popular with children all over the world. Follow the steps below to create your own unique tag game to practise moving and dodging skills.

1 Think of a theme and a name

What are the children learning in class at the moment? What topic are they studying? What are their interests?

Examples:

- Roman Tag: Gladiators are being chased by lions.
- Harry Potter Tag: Gryffindor v Slytherin.

2 The three basic rules

Set the following three basic rules. Choose one of the options listed below for each rule or invent your own.

Rule 1: How will the taggers tag the others?

- By touching them on their back or with a noodle.
- By throwing a bib at them.

Rule 2: What happens when they are tagged?
Those who are tagged must:

- freeze and await release by a teammate
- leave the area, complete a task and then re-join
- switch roles with the tagger
- link arms with the tagger and join the tagging team.

Rule 3: How do you win the game? Or how does the game finish?

- The taggers freeze everyone.
- Those being chased manage to steal all the treasure.
- There is a time limit of three minutes.

3 Spaces and zones

What space, boundaries and zones will you use? You might consider:

- a jail area where those who are tagged go to (to await release by a teammate)
- a safe zone where they can't be tagged
- a space to get into and out of during the game, for example a dragon's den to enter.

4 The extras

Decide whether it will be a team game or an individual game:

- **Individual:** Everyone against everyone else.
- **Two teams:** See Treasure Tag on page 30.
- **Multi-teams:** See Super Mario™ Battle on page 89.

Will any of the children have a special role? For example:

- Children with blue noodles are 'ice bandits' who freeze people; children with red noodles are 'fire warriors' who can release those who are frozen.
- In Star Wars™ Tag, each team has a 'Skywalker' who wears a white bib and cannot be tagged but is the only person who can free their teammates.

How will players move around the space? They could run, crawl or hop.

Will you need any equipment? Think about balls to bounce, treasure to steal, and bibs as tails.

Aim

To time a jump
over a moving
obstacle.

Set-up

Grouping:
Pairs.

Equipment needed:
One noodle per pair.

Space needed:
Any.

Noodle skipping

A pair activity to practise the timing
of jumps for skipping.

How to facilitate the game

1 Demonstrate the game. One child holds the end of a noodle and stands to the side of their partner. They start with the noodle on the floor in front of their partner and slide the noodle so their partner must jump over it. They then lift the noodle up behind their partner, over their partner's head and down to the floor in front of them, before sliding it for their partner to jump over again.

2 Play. Ask the children to find a partner, get a noodle and begin.

3 Add scoring. This is a collaborative game in which the two children need to work together to succeed. Once the children have had a chance to get used to the activity, you can challenge them to count how many successful jumps they can make in a row. They can then work to beat their own score, or to see which pair in the class gets the highest score.

Adaptations

For successful pairs or older classes, you could explore a variety of different kinds of jumps, for example:

- hopping on one foot

- jumping from one foot to the other foot

- jumping in a pattern: one foot, two feet, one foot, etc.

Assessment for learning

This game introduces the skills needed for skipping. The noodle moves more slowly than a rope, so this version allows the children to practise the timing of their jumps with a greater chance of success. Successful pairs will usually have worked out a rhythm, with a consistent circular pattern of the noodle making the timing of jumps easier. It might be useful to demonstrate this rhythm with a pair of children who can do it well.

- How should you land after your jump so you are ready to jump again soon? (Answer: light on your feet, gently.)

- How high do you need to jump to get over the noodle? (You can help children have more success by showing that it is easier to jump over the noodle as it slides along the floor rather than jumping while it's at knee height.)

See page 112 for a photo of this game in action with a KS1 class.

Volcanoes and craters

*Half the class play against the other half
in this high-intensity quick starter.*

How to facilitate the game

1 **Show the area.** Spread the cones out over the area, making sure that some are the right way up (volcanoes) and some are the wrong way up (craters).

2 **Split the class in half.** There's no need to take a long time doing this. Just separate the children into two roughly equal-sized teams.

3 **Explain the rules.** One team are the volcanoes, and they need to move around the area and flip as many cones as they can upside down. The other team are the craters and they need to move around the area and flip as many cones as they can the right way up.

4 **Play.** Make sure both teams know their role, and then start. Play for two minutes, then 'Freeze!' and quickly count the cones to determine the winning team.

5 **Introduce movements.** Play the game again but this time children need to jump over the cone and land before they can flip the cone. Use a whiteboard to write down a variety of different types of jumps and landings the children could do. Assign a different type of jump for each cone colour. For example:

  a. **Red cone:** Hop with one foot over the cone.
  b. **Yellow cone:** Do a two-footed bunny hop over the cone.
  c. **Green cone:** Jump with two feet and land on one foot.

Assessment for learning

Deliver this game in short, sharp bursts. It is tiring for the children as there are no rests, and you should be aiming for good technique rather than exhaustion.

- Which type of jump and landing was most difficult for you? Why?

- What did you need to do well in order to move around the area without bumping into others? (Answer: look around before moving, move with caution.)

 Aim

*To practise a
variety of jumps,
hops and landings.*

Set-up

Grouping:
A whole class split
into two large teams.

Equipment needed:
Lots of small cones (you'll
need more cones than
children). A whiteboard.

Space needed:
Any.

*Take a child out of the activity to provide feedback, check
understanding or suggest a challenge. The activity can
continue for the rest of the children while you do this.*

Aim
To change speed and direction to get past defenders.

Set-up

Grouping:
Groups of five.

Equipment needed:
Cones or spots to create a circle on the floor.

Space needed:
Any.

Ring of fire

Move to create a space to escape.

How to facilitate the game

1 Show the area. Set up a circle on the floor, using six or seven spots or cones. The size of the circle will depend on the age and ability of the children and may need amending as the activity progresses. The diameter of the circle should be approximately the same length as four children holding hands, stretched out in a line.

2 Demonstrate the game. Ask four children to stand around the edge (circumference) of the circle, facing towards the middle. These children must guard the circle and make sure no one gets out, but they can only move side to side along the edge of the circle. Another child starts in the middle of the circle and needs to move to escape out of the circle without getting tagged by someone on the edge.

3 Play. Ask children to find groups of five and set up their circles.

Adaptations

Adjust the size of the circle if needed: a larger circle will make it easier for the person in the middle to escape, and a smaller circle will make it harder.

↓ You could try having two children in the middle of the circle instead of one, both trying to escape. This should make it easier for them to escape.

↑ You could progress so the child in the middle needs to escape out, and then also find a way back in.

Assessment for learning

The child in the middle should start to notice that the children on the edge of the circle will move in response to their own movements within the circle. Sometimes, even turning to face a different direction will result in movements of children on the edge of the circle. The questions below may help them notice this and help them work out how they might use quick changes of speed and direction to create spaces to escape without being tagged.

● What happens to the children on the edge of the circle when the person in the middle moves to try to escape?

● How might the middle person move in one direction so that they create a space on the opposite side of the circle? What do they then need to do well in order to escape?

 Cross-curricular link

This is a great activity to apply the vocabulary of circle measurements, such as radius, diameter and circumference.

Getaway tag

A racing and chasing game involving stealth and quick acceleration.

How to facilitate the game

1 Demonstrate the game. Ask for a volunteer to demonstrate with you. They will be the chaser and start by facing a wall (or you could use a line on the floor). The chaser is not allowed to look behind them. Ask for another volunteer. They will be the racer and must sneak up on the chaser, tap them on the back and run away. When the chaser is tapped, they can spin round and chase the racer, aiming to catch up and tag them. Put a cone or use a line on the floor on the other side of the area to denote a safe space that the racer is trying to reach without being tagged.

2 Split the class. This game is arranged so that half the class are chasers and half are racers. You can do this quickly by dividing the class roughly down the middle.

3 Play. Line the chasers up against one wall or boundary. They should spread out so that several racers can safely initiate a chase at the same time. Once a chase is finished – either because the racer has reached the safe area or they have been tagged by the chaser – the chaser resumes their position on the boundary and gets ready for the next round. The racer can then choose to tap the same chaser again or choose a different chaser.

Adaptations

↑ When the racer gets to the safe area, they then need to make it back to the boundary, past the chaser, without being tagged.

Assessment for learning

This racing game should be played over a short distance.

- What do you need to do with your body in order to start moving quickly? (Answer: lean forward, be low to the floor, pump the arms, be on the balls of your feet.)

- How might the racer approach and tap the chaser to give them the best chance of accelerating away quickly? (Answer: if they approach backwards, with their body already facing towards the safe area, that will help them get away more quickly.)

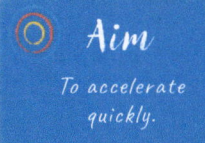

Aim

To accelerate quickly.

Set-up

Grouping:
Whole class together.

Equipment needed:
None.

Space needed:
Any.

Top TIP

To practise jumping or hopping skills, this game could be adapted so children cannot run during the chase but must move in a different way.

Aim

To jump and land in a variety of different ways.

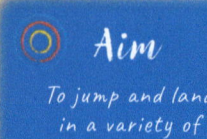

Set-up

Grouping:
Pairs or groups of three.

Equipment needed:
One hoop per group.

Space needed:
Any.

Hoop jump

A kicking and jumping game using a hoop.

How to facilitate the game

1 Demonstrate the game. Ask for a volunteer and send them to stand a few metres away. Ask for another volunteer and put a hoop flat on the floor next to them. The child with the hoop will kick the hoop across the floor towards their partner. Their partner will see if they can jump into the moving hoop as it comes to them.

2 Play. Tell the children to pair up or make a group of three and see if they can kick and jump successfully.

3 Add in scoring. Write the scoring system on a whiteboard while the children practise. Bring the children in and show them the scoring and then send them out again to see how many points they can score together.

The scoring system:

- Two feet jump and land (one point)

- Two feet jump, one foot lands (two points)

- One foot jumps, other foot lands (three points)

- One foot hops (four points)

Assessment for learning

The scoring system should encourage the children to try a variety of different jumps and landings. You could also encourage them to come up with their own 'five-point' jump.

- Why is it harder to hop than to jump with two feet?

- How do your hands and arms help you to jump and land?

Cross-curricular link

Of all the animals, dolphins are able to jump the highest distance (seven metres) and kangaroos can jump the longest distance (13.5 metres).

Work in groups and use a measuring tape to measure this out.

Robin Hood

Steal from the rich, give to the poor and escape King John's soldiers.

How to facilitate the game

1 Show the area. This game could be played in a hall or a playground. You may want to mark out the boundaries so that the children know where the playing area stops.

2 Demonstrate the game. Most of the class are in Robin Hood's gang. They have stolen treasure from the rich and are running away to give it to the poor. They each hold a bib (the treasure) in their hand and need to try to get away from King John's soldiers. Each soldier has a (cannon)ball that they dribble with their feet. The soldier needs to kick the ball so it hits one of Robin Hood's gang below knee height. If they succeed in this, they take the bib treasure and join Robin Hood's gang. The child who is hit with the ball becomes a soldier, using the ball to try to get one of Robin Hood's gang.

3 Play. Choose some children to start as soldiers. In a class of 30, about ten soldiers makes a perfect ratio. Give them each a ball. Make sure the rest of the class have a bib each.

Adaptations

Instead of dribbling the ball with their feet, children could bounce it like in basketball or carry it like in rugby. They could throw or roll the ball, instead of kicking it, to hit one of Robin Hood's gang.

↓ Mark out a square to be Sherwood Forest – a 'safe zone' where Robin Hood's people can't get caught by the soldiers.

Assessment for learning

The main teaching will be directed at the Robin Hood role and how they move and dodge to avoid the soldiers and their balls. Here are some questions that you could use to help children grow their confidence and ability to dodge moving obstacles.

● What should you be looking at as you move around? (Answer: the ball.)

● How do you get yourself ready to jump or dodge the ball? (Answer: be on the balls of your feet, low to the ground and ready to move.)

Classroom debate

Show the class some videos of Olympic and Paralympic events: 100 metres, 5,000 metres, long jump and high jump. Ask: which of these do you think is the hardest event?

Aim

To jump and dodge over and around moving footballs.

Set-up

Grouping:
Whole class together.

Equipment needed:
One bib per child, plus ten footballs (or other balls). Optional: four spots or cones to make a safe zone on the floor.

Space needed:
Any.

Ninja warrior

Create and explore jump-racing
obstacle courses for young ninjas.

Aim

To jump over,
around and through
an assortment
of obstacles.

Set-up

Grouping:
Groups of three to five.

Equipment needed:
Hoops, cones, balls,
hurdles, benches, mats
and anything else from
the PE cupboard that
could be used safely
as obstacles.

Space needed:
Any.

How to facilitate the game

1 Set the task. Tell the children they are going to create their own obstacle course for other children to explore or race through. Explain that you'd particularly like them to include obstacles to practise their jumping skills. Show them the equipment and area that they can use. It would be a good idea to introduce some rules, perhaps on a whiteboard, for example: you must work together, you must share ideas and you have 20 minutes to complete the task.

2 Play. Divide the class into groups and designate an area for them to use. You may now need to help them share ideas, use the equipment sensibly and design a course that includes a range of jumping opportunities. Encourage the children to test their own courses often.

3 Race! Leave time towards the end of the lesson for children to try each other's courses. This could work well by leaving one child at each course to explain and demonstrate how it works while others move around to try other courses.

Assessment for learning

In this lesson, learning will mostly happen through physical exploration. However, it might be worthwhile reflecting on the variety of jumping techniques they have practised and their experience of using them in a race.

- What was the most difficult obstacle you had to jump through, over or around?

- What is the difference between jumping for length and jumping for height? Which do you find easier?

The activity could be done as a follow-the-leader game rather than a race.

Top TIP

This game provides a great opportunity to use your playground equipment. Many schools have climbing frames and other interesting equipment in their playground. You could encourage the children to include these in their course design.

The clock strikes twelve

A glorious striking and fielding game with multiple runners and plenty of action.

How to facilitate the game

1 Show the area. The whole class will play the game together on the same court. The court has a hoop in the middle, with 12 tennis balls inside. Around the hoop are four tall cones, in a square shape, each about five metres from the hoop (adjust the exact distance according to the ability of the class).

2 Demonstrate the game. Show the game with the first team of five players.

- The first team of five players will start by taking up their positions: there are four batters, one on each of the tall cones, and one bowler in the hoop. In this game, the bowler and the batters are on the same team. This makes it different from other striking and fielding games.

- The rest of the class are the fielders and position themselves anywhere they like outside of the square made by the tall cones. The bowler will bowl the 12 tennis balls to any of the batters, in any order, whenever they like. They can bowl with a throw or a roll.

- Each batter can choose to strike the ball with a noodle, a tennis racket or their palm, or kick it with their foot.

- Once a batter has struck the ball, they must run clockwise around the square of tall cones. If they make it back to their own cone before the fielders return the ball there, they get a point for their team (if they don't, they return to the cone and can have another turn).

- Fielders cannot move with the ball but must throw the ball instead.

- The maximum score for a team is therefore 12 points.

3 Play. Once the first five players have had their turn, choose the next team of five players and so on. Each team can keep their own score.

Assessment for learning

The trick of this game is for the bowler to catch the fielders off-guard by bowling two or three balls in quick succession to different batters. This gives the fielders a problem as they need to retrieve multiple balls at once and remember which ball needs to be retrieved to which cone.

However, our teaching will focus on the running movements and reactions of the batters.

- When do you need to start running?

- What will help you to move faster? (Answer: quick start, pumping arms, sustained effort.)

Aim

To run for speed while avoiding other people.

Set-up

Grouping:
Teams of five.

Equipment needed:
Four tall cones, four noodles, four tennis rackets, one hoop and 12 tennis balls.

Space needed:
Any.

The Clock Strikes Twelve

Aim

To practise starting, stopping and changing direction.

Set-up

Grouping:
Teams of four or five.

Equipment needed:
One ball per game.
Lines or spots on the floor to show the boundaries of the pitch.

Space needed:
Any.

Touch rugby

An exciting Key Stage 2 team game with plenty of sudden starts, stops and changes of direction.

How to facilitate the game

1 Show the pitch. Each pitch will be a small rectangle. You can fit three pitches side by side across a netball court.

2 Introduce the basic rules. One team starts with the ball in the middle of the pitch. They pick the ball up from the floor to begin the game. The aim of the game is to get the ball to the opponents' end of the pitch and touch it to the floor. This is called a 'try'. In order to move the ball up the pitch they can run with the ball in their hands. The ball may be thrown and caught between children on the same team, but the ball must be thrown backwards or sideways, not forwards.

3 Practise. Let each team have a ball and practise how they might move up the pitch by running forward and passing backwards or sideways.

4 Explain how to win possession. At the start of the game, the opposition team must retreat to their own end of the pitch. As soon as the ball is picked up, the opposition may come forward. The opposition team can win possession of the ball if:

- they are able to intercept a pass
- they can tag an opponent who is holding the ball on their back
- the opposing team makes a forward pass.

When they win possession of the ball, the opposing team must retreat to their end of the pitch before play begins again.

5 Play. Divide the class into teams and send them to a pitch to play. You may need to go round and clear up any confusion about the rules to make sure everyone understands how the game works.

Adaptations

↓ You could play this game with a small rugby ball. It will be easier to play with a round ball to start with though (as it is easier to throw accurately).

↓ Another useful adaptation is to play the game on a wide pitch rather than a narrow one. This will make it easier to score as there is more space to attack.

↑ An additional rule (if you get to this stage) is that players can kick the ball forward and a teammate can run ahead and get the ball as long as they are behind the kicker when the ball is kicked.

Assessment for learning

This game may take a while for children to get the hang of. If you are successful, some children will love the game and continue to play in the playground during breaks. The beauty of the game is in its fast movements and quick starts and stops to pretend to go one way but change and go another.

- What kinds of movements are most successful in this game?

- What do you need to do well in order to start and stop quickly? (Answer: be low to the floor, use your arms to pump for starts and push off from the balls of your feet for stops.)

Looking forward to next month's theme on defending skills, the red team offer a really good example of team defending. Two players force the player wide and block passes to teammates, while a third player offers cover and balance.

The whole-part-whole lesson design

In the whole-part-whole method of teaching, the lesson starts with the full version of a game (the 'whole'). This allows the teacher to assess the ability of the children in relation to the learning intentions of the lesson. Children who are struggling and those who are ahead can be identified.

The lesson then moves to an activity that is smaller and contains lots of repetitions of specific, intended learning (the 'part').

This mini game allows the children to focus on a specific aspect of the whole game and provides the teacher with opportunities to develop children's ability, confidence and understanding in the specific, targeted area.

After this, the session moves back to the 'whole' game again. This encourages the practice and progress made in the 'part' section of the lesson to be applied back to the whole-game context.

Example

Learning intention: To move and jump to receive a pass

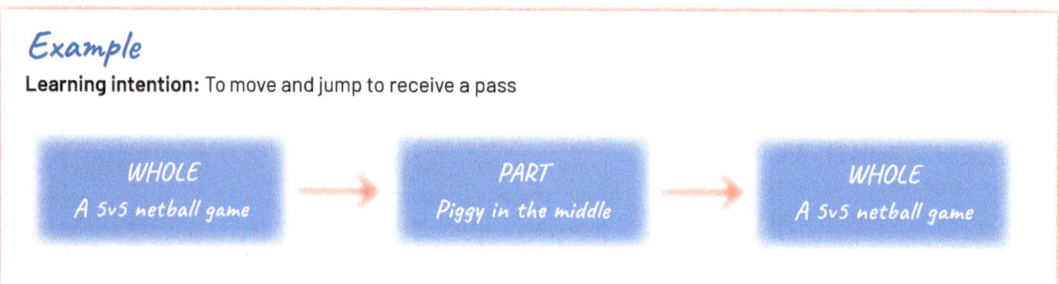

The whole-part-whole method may be useful for primary PE because:

- It means the lesson is based on games. Games are engaging for children, and children's behaviours may be more enthusiastic and positive because of this.

- The 'whole' game at the start allows the teacher to observe and assess the ability, confidence and understanding of the children, and plan the 'part' section based on these observations.

- The 'whole' game at the start provides a context for the practice of skills in the 'part' section that follows. This may mean better attention and focus from children in the 'part' section as they understand why they are practising the techniques and skills.

- The 'whole' game at the end provides an opportunity to apply the techniques and skills from the 'part' section in a larger format of game.

For an example of the whole-part-whole method, see The Great Fire of London on the next page.

The Great Fire of London

A whole-class jumping and dodging game with a fiery theme and using the whole-part-whole lesson structure.

Aim

To jump and land for distance and accuracy.

Set-up

Grouping:
Whole class together.

Equipment needed:
Roughly 40 floor spots to make a jumping area. 24 cones to create 'gates' around the outside of the area.

Space needed:
Any.

How to facilitate the game

Whole

1 Show the area. The area needed is a large rectangle. This rectangle is going to be London. There are two 'gates' along each short side and four on each long side. Gates are two cones or markers about two metres apart from each other which children can travel through to get in and out of London. In the middle of London (inside the rectangle), there are lots of houses on fire. These are denoted by spots on the floor. Scatter the spots across the area, so they are close enough to each other for the children to jump from one to another (for a class of 30, you'll need about 40 spots).

2 Tell the story. Tell the children the story of the fire and how it spread from a bakery on Pudding Lane in 1666. The children are going to be firefighters, putting out fires and escaping from the city. They put out fires by jumping on the spots in the middle of London, and they escape the city out of any of the gates.

3 Play. Challenge the children to jump successfully across four (or more) spots before escaping.

4 Add the fire. After the children have had a go at the activity and have understood the story and the set-up, you can add in some extra challenge. Explain that the fire has now spread, and it is much harder to escape from the city. Ask some children to be fires. They should each guard a set of gates and try to tag anyone who is trying to escape. If a firefighter gets caught by a flame, they switch places with the flame.

Part

5 For the 'part' section of the lesson, we will focus on the jumping aspect of the game. All children should be in the area filled with spots and the aim of this part of the lesson is to give them lots of practice at jumping and landing. The children should aim to jump from one spot to another successfully so they don't touch the floor.

6 You could pair up the children and make this a follow-the-leader activity. You may need to

The Great Fire of London

move some spots around the area to make some gaps larger than others. You could add a rule that it is OK to touch the ground once between spots (this allows children to cover longer distances between spots).

Whole

7 Go back to the 'whole' section as played at the beginning. Challenge the children to make longer sequences of different types of jump in the middle area before escaping. Keep increasing the gaps between some spots if extra challenge is needed.

Assessment for learning

The teaching and learning focus should be on the jumping techniques used by the children when they are moving from spot to spot.

● What do you do with your body that helps you to jump further? (Answer: bend to prepare for a jump, swing arms upwards when jumping.)

● What do you need to do well to land properly? (Answer: land in a balanced position with bent knees and hips.)

 Cross-curricular link

The Great Fire of London was eventually put out because the wind died down and because soldiers from the Tower of London used gunpowder and explosions to create spaces to stop the fire spreading.

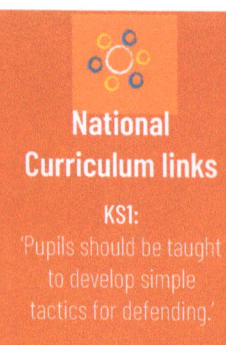

National Curriculum links

KS1:
'Pupils should be taught to develop simple tactics for defending.'

KS2:
'Pupils should be taught to apply basic principles suitable for defending.'

March

Defending skills

An introduction to defending skills

Spring is in the air as we start to consider how to teach defending. The National Curriculum mentions 'tactics' for KS1 and 'principles' for KS2 and these terms can be scary for teachers who are not familiar with them. In the games this month, we help teachers and children to acquire defending knowledge and skills through an exploration of space and movement in simple, engaging games.

In Goodminton (page 140), which is a 'net or wall' game, we explore how to defend a space and how we might aim our shots over the net so we have as much time as possible to get to the best defending position.

In Field of Dreams (page 144), which is a 'striking and fielding' game, we explore how defenders (fielders) need to be ready to move quickly and how they might move to defend and cover the areas that opponents are trying to hit the ball into.

In Breakout (page 143), which is an 'invasion' game, we explore how we might move to protect a target or goal, how we can provide 'cover' to support another defender, and how we might try to steal the ball from the attackers so we can counter-attack.

When playing attack versus defence games, some children may be less excited by the defending roles. If this is the case, try calling them 'counter-attackers' instead of defenders. This change of vocabulary helps them realise that their job is to win the ball and go and attack, which is more exciting than simply defending.

Key skills

Simple tactics for defending (KS1)

Move to

- 🔴 protect the goal or the space that the attackers are trying to get to
- 🟠 be ready and react quickly when the attackers move or the ball moves
- 🔵 slow down or stop the attackers (in invasion games only)

Basic principles suitable for defending (KS2)

Move to

- 🔴 defend spaces to make it harder for the attackers
- 🟠 'cover' and 'support' other defenders on your team
- 🔵 apply 'pressure' to the ball (in invasion games only)

In Field of Dreams (page 144), the defenders will need to decide where to stand to best cover the area so they can retrieve the ball quickly.

A questioning matrix for defending skills in invasion games

Questioning is an important part of teaching. This questioning matrix includes a variety of example questions that you might ask individuals or groups during games in order to check or share understanding about defending. The questions are separated into those concerning simple tactics (KS1) and those which involve deeper thinking about the principles of defending (KS2). Notice also how questions in the top left of the matrix ('What does...?', 'Where was...?') are less complex than those questions in the bottom right of the matrix ('How might...?'). Teachers can use the matrix to select appropriate initial and follow-up questions.

Note how the complexity level of the questions increases towards the bottom right of the matrix	KS1: Simple defending tactics		KS2: Basic defending principles	
	What? Where? When? DESCRIPTION	Who? Which? CHOICE	Why? REASON	How? MEANING
Is? Does? Has? Was? DESCRIPTION	Where is your opponent trying to get to?	Who is the most dangerous attacker?	Why has your team struggled to defend so far?	How does it help you to slow down as you approach the attacker?
Can? POSSIBILITY	What can you do to stop the attacker scoring the goal?	Who can score easily if they get the ball?	Why can the attacker score more easily if they are closer to the goal?	How can you try to force the attacker away from the goal?
Should? OPINION	When should you get back to help your team defend?	Which should you do: block the attacker or mark their partner?	Why should you be ready to move at all times?	How should you defend when you are defending as a pair with someone else?
Would? Could? PROBABILITY	Where could you move to cover the area behind your team?	Which would be easiest to defend: a large area or a small area?	Why would you want to win the ball back near their goal?	How could you stop them from playing a forward pass?
Will? PREDICTION Might? IMAGINATION	When will the attacker try to get past you?	Who might be in the best position to defend the goal?	Why will you need to get back quickly to help your team?	How might you trap the attacker in the corner and not let them escape?

Defending: individual challenges for invasion games

When it comes to understanding and application of defending skills in games there will likely be a wide variety of abilities within your class. One way to deal with this is to consider providing individual children with specific challenges. Some individual challenges might be simple and straightforward and help children who are struggling to focus on one key aspect of defending. Other challenges might be more complex and engage talented defenders with a focused, higher-level challenge.

These challenges can be given to children in games. You can do this in a variety of ways:

- You could call someone over while the game is going on and give them a challenge before sending them back in to see if they can fulfil it.

- You can make challenge cards for defending (to keep in your PE cupboard). Hand these out to individuals or teams during games.

- You could have a whiteboard with the challenges written on and children can come over and choose which to attempt next.

The challenges

- Be patient and calm when defending – don't 'jump in' to a tackle.

- Try to recover quickly 'goal-side' as soon as your team loses the ball.

- Try to slow your opponent down and force them away from the goal.

- Try to put pressure on the player with the ball when you see an opportunity to do so.

- Try to intercept a pass and start an attack.

- Try to defend patiently when in a 1v1 situation and don't let your opponent get past you.

- Choose who you are going to mark and stick with them so they can't receive a pass.

- As a goalkeeper, try to move towards the attacker when they are through on goal.

- As a goalkeeper, try to come out and intercept passes before the opposing attacker receives the ball.

Key vocabulary for defending in invasion games

- **1v1:** A situation in a game where there is one defender directly defending against one attacker.
- **Cover:** To move to help defend a space.
- **Force away from goal:** To block the attacker's path to the goal and ensure the attacker moves away from the goal.
- **Goal-side:** A position between the ball and the goal you are defending.
- **Intercept:** To steal the ball while it is being passed between attackers.
- **Mark:** To take responsibility for ensuring a specific attacker doesn't receive the ball.

- **Pressure:** To move towards an attacker who has the ball and block their forward path.
- **Recover:** To move into a 'goal-side' position.
- **Side-on:** To position your body so you are sideways to the ball, allowing you to turn your head to see both the ball and the goal you are defending.
- **Tackle:** To win the ball while it is being controlled by an opponent.
- **Through on goal:** When an attacker has broken through the defence and only has the goalkeeper to beat.

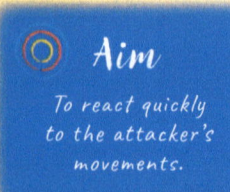

Aim
To react quickly to the attacker's movements.

Set-up

Grouping:
Pairs.

Equipment needed:
Two spots or cones to mark out the area.

Space needed:
Any.

Dragon v shadow

Protect the treasure before the dragon steals it in this quick racing game.

How to facilitate the game

1 Show the area. Set up two cones about three metres apart. The two cones have an imaginary line joining them.

2 Demonstrate the game. Ask a pair to come and demonstrate. They should stand facing each other either side of the imaginary line. One of the pair is the dragon who must try to get to one of the cones to steal it by picking it up with their hand. The shadow must keep up with the dragon, and if the shadow puts their foot next to the cone, then this gives the cone special protection and it can't be stolen. Neither the dragon nor the shadow can cross the imaginary line between the cones. If a cone is stolen by the dragon, the children replace the cone and restart.

3 Play. The children can find their own partner, get their own cones and set up their own area. Make sure you change dragon and shadow roles often. Ask the children to keep score if they want.

Adaptations

↓ If you have a fast child playing against a slower child, this mismatch can affect engagement and learning for both children. You can solve this by changing partners every so often: ask those who won their games to go and find someone else who also won, and those who lost their games to go and find someone else who also lost.

Assessment for learning

We will be working with the shadows in this game as they are the defenders. These questions may help them consider how to deal with attackers who like to try to trick them with quick changes of speed or direction.

● Who was the most difficult shadow you played against? What did they do well?

● What might you do to keep up with a very tricky dragon? (Answers might be: Getting low to the floor, knees bent, staying on your toes, being ready to go.)

Piggy in the middle

Win by touching the ball in this modified version of a classic game.

How to facilitate the game

1 Demonstrate the game. Ask three children to join you to demonstrate the game to the class. Two of the children form a pair. Give them a ball to keep between them. They must throw and catch the ball and get a point for each successful throw and catch. The ball must be thrown so that it remains below shoulder height. The third child will be the 'piggy in the middle', and they must try to intercept the ball while it is being thrown. If they can touch the ball when it is in the air being thrown between the other players, then they are released from being the piggy and swap roles with one of the other children.

2 Play. Ask the children to form groups of three, choose a ball and find their own space to play.

Adaptations

These adaptations make it easier for the piggy to intercept the ball.

↓ If the pair of children are finding it too easy, you can challenge them to get double points if the ball bounces when it is passed between them.

↓ Reduce the space between the pair and restrict them to a specific zone.

↓ You could allow the piggy to swap roles if they touch the ball when it is in the hands of one of the others. This may force them to speed up their throws.

Assessment for learning

In order to intercept the ball, it helps if the piggy stands 'side-on' so they can see both their opponents just by turning their head. The first question below focuses on this important aspect of defending. The second question considers how a slow or inaccurate pass between the two opponents gives the piggy a chance to put pressure on the opponent receiving the ball.

● How does it help you to be able to see both of the others? How might you position yourself so you can see them both?

● When do you have the best chance of chasing the ball and touching it before it reaches them?

Set-up

Grouping:
Groups of three.

Equipment needed:
One ball
(or another object suitable for throwing)
per group.

Space needed:
Any.

The defender (the piggy in the middle) should try to take up a sideways position so they can turn their head to switch between seeing the ball and seeing the target player. This should help them to intercept a pass.

Slam

Be ready to catch
a bouncing ball.

How to facilitate the game

1 Demonstrate the game. You will need a pair of children to demonstrate. Put a hoop on the floor. One of the children must throw the ball into the hoop so it bounces out of the hoop. The other child needs to try to catch the ball after it bounces out of the hoop and prevent it from bouncing a second time. They get a point if they can stop the ball from hitting the ground outside of the hoop.

2 Play. Ask the children to find a partner and play. They have five turns each before swapping over. They should count their score.

Adaptations

↑ For older classes, it can be useful to progress this activity so that each child serves and strikes the ball with their palm, rather than throwing it into the hoop. This is a good skill development for games like volleyball and tennis.

↑ If you have enough equipment, you could use two hoops (next to each other) and two balls. The children stand opposite each other, with the two hoops between them. At the same time, each child serves a ball into a different hoop, then they race to retrieve the ball their opponent served. (See the photo on page 136.)

Assessment for learning

As this game progresses, the children should work out that they can 'slam' the ball into the ground and make it more difficult to catch. Our teaching must focus on the catcher, as they are the defender in this situation. Our questions and discussion should aim to help them reflect on how they decide where to position themselves to have the best chance of catching the ball and scoring a point.

● How do you know how far from the hoop to position yourself?

● What clues does the thrower give away that help you to decide where to stand?

Cross-curricular link

Before you start this game, introduce a selection of balls of different sizes, weights and textures. Ask the children which they think will bounce highest and which will be easiest to catch.

Play the game. Were the children correct?

Aim
To move to respond to the attacker's intentions and to the flight of the ball.

Set-up
Grouping:
Pairs or groups of three.

Equipment needed:
One hoop and one ball per pair.

Space needed:
Any.

Superglue

Pairs of children stick to each other like glue in this two-against-two game.

Aim

To practise blocking and marking an opponent and to explore defending as a pair.

Set-up

Grouping:
Pairs (with some teams of three if you have extra children).

Equipment needed:
One ball per game and some cones to denote scoring zones.

Space needed:
Each court hosts two pairs of children playing against each other. Seven small courts are needed for a class of 30.

How to facilitate the game

1 **Show the area.** Set up two small rectangles with cones or floor spots. These rectangles should be just a few metres away from each other and will be the scoring areas for the game. To score a point, you need to catch the ball in the scoring area. The game could be played as netball, handball or basketball (or any other invasion game).

2 **Demonstrate the game.** Ask for four children to help demonstrate and put them into two teams of two players each (Teams A and B). Match players up between teams, so Player 1 from Team A is matched with Player 1 from Team B, and Player 2 from Team A is matched with Player 2 from Team B. The players are matched up so they can only mark and tackle each other. Play for a minute so the rest of the class can watch and see how the game works.

3 **Play.** Let the children set up their games and begin. You may need to swap some pairs between games so you have more even contests. You can do this without stopping the whole class; just ask the pairs to come and see you and send them to their new opponents.

Assessment for learning

Children are defenders in this game when the other team has the ball. They need to understand how their role changes depending on which opponent has the ball. If their direct opponent has the ball, their job is to block the path to goal and to slow the opponent down. If their teammate's opponent has the ball, they need to mark their own opponent. When marking someone, they should stand between the opponent and the goal they are trying to get to ('goal-side' of the opponent) and be ready to jump in to intercept a pass if possible.

● What is your job when your direct opponent has the ball? What is your job when your teammate's opponent has the ball?

● When you are marking someone, where is the best position to stand and why? When might you steal or intercept a pass between opponents?

Superglue

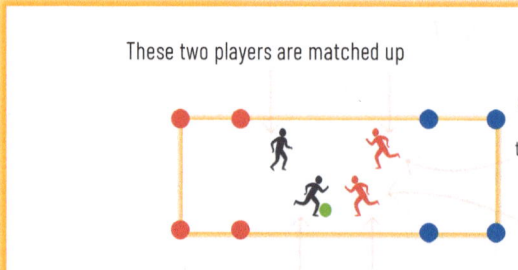

These two players are matched up

This defender marks their opponent and covers the space behind their teammate in case they get beaten

This defender applies pressure on the ball

These two players are matched up

Three and in

An updated version of this classic children's football game.

How to facilitate the game

1 **Explain the game.** This is a familiar football game but it could be played as any invasion game, so perhaps the children could choose themselves which game to play. Each group has a goalkeeper who protects the goal. If the goalkeeper gets the ball, they throw it back into the playing area. The other players are competing against each other and all need to try to score in the same goal. The first player to score three goals goes in goal for the next round (or that player can choose who gets to go in goal next).

2 **Play.** The children can choose their own groups and set up their own goals.

Adaptations

↑ There is an interesting progression for older classes where a target is placed far away from the goal and the goalkeeper has the chance to try to dribble the ball to the target when they save a shot or intercept a pass. If they make it successfully to the target

without being tackled, they can come out of goal and they get to choose the next goalkeeper.

Assessment for learning

The defenders in this game are the players without the ball, so this includes the goalkeeper and the other players who are trying to win the ball back and score. The players trying to win the ball back need to position themselves between the ball and the goal ('goal-side'). They need to get there as quickly as possible to block the path of the player with the ball (the attacker). Once there, they need to stop the attacker from shooting at the goal and slow the attacker down by getting in their way.

● When you lose the ball, where is the most useful place to move to straight away?

● What is your job when you are between the player with the ball and the goal?

Aim

To recover 'goal-side' as early as possible and to block the attacker's path to goal.

Set-up

Grouping:
Groups of three to five.

Equipment needed:
One ball per group, and some goals or cones to make a target.

Space needed:
Each group needs a small space only and group areas can overlap.

Top TIP

Although the traditional playground game is called 'three and in', you may like to change the game to 'one and in' as this will speed up changes in goalkeeper and may keep children more engaged for longer.

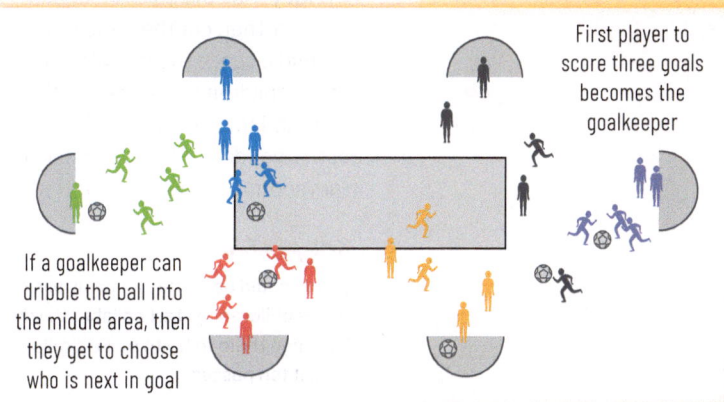

Three and In

First player to score three goals becomes the goalkeeper

If a goalkeeper can dribble the ball into the middle area, then they get to choose who is next in goal

Goodminton

*Like badminton,
but even better.*

Aim

To move in an
area so you can
cover and defend
the space.

Set-up

Grouping:
Pairs or groups of four.

Equipment needed:
One balloon, some dry
rice, and four cones
or spots per pair.
One badminton
racket per child.
A net, bench, or cones
to make a dividing line
on each court.

Space needed:
Each game takes place
on a small court.

How to facilitate the game

1 Prepare the balloons. Before the lesson, blow up enough balloons for one per pair. It's also worth blowing up a few extra in case any pop during the game.

2 Show the court. Each game should take place on a court with side lines. There should be a centre line such as a net, a bench or a line on the floor. In the far corners of each court, place a cone or floor spot.

3 Demonstrate the game. Ask for a pair to demonstrate and give them each a badminton racket. Explain that the game is competitive and they are playing against each other. They will play a rally with the balloon, and they will score if they can land the balloon so it touches one of the cones (or spots) on their partner's side of the court.

4 Play. Ask the children to find a partner, get their equipment and find a space to play. Allow time for the children to get used to the game and to start to identify the key tactics needed to stop their partner from scoring easily.

Adaptations

↓ You could begin this game by asking the children to start collaboratively. Challenge them to try to make a rally of at least ten passes.

↓ Younger children could use their hands rather than a racket.

↑ For children who are ready, substitute the balloon for a shuttlecock.

↑ The cones don't necessarily need to be in the far corners of the court. You could have each child position the cones on their partner's side of the court. This gets them thinking about what is easiest to attack and hardest to defend and may enhance game understanding.

If you're short on space, you could play 'doubles' where there are two players on each team. If you do this, have three cones on each side of the court instead of two.

Assessment for learning

We will focus our questioning on the defending skills needed to prevent your partner from scoring easily.

● When is it easiest to score a point?

● How and when do you need to move so you can protect both the cones?

● How can you make it difficult for your partner to win a point?

Top TIP

Before you blow up each balloon, put a little bit of rice in it. This will mean the balloon makes a lovely sound when it is hit. It will also be a bit heavier and move faster in the air.

Not all the courts need to be the same.
Use whatever equipment and space you
have available. Be inventive!

Family tail tag

A whole-class tag game which introduces principles of defending.

Aim

To work with other defenders to trap attackers in small spaces (like corners).

Set-up

Grouping:
Whole class together.

Equipment needed:
Each child will need a bib tucked into their waistband or pocket as a tail.

Space needed:
Any.

How to facilitate the game

1 Show the area. Defending principles relating to space are redundant if children don't stick to the boundaries. Show the children the area shape, size, corners and side lines.

2 Explain the game. The game is a simple one that the children probably already play at playtime. Everyone has a tail (a bib tucked into their waistband or pocket). There are two taggers who start with no tail, and they need to steal the tails from the others. Once a tail is stolen, it is returned to a safe area off the pitch. The child who has had their tail stolen joins the team of taggers, which gets larger and larger until there is only one child left with a tail.

3 Play. Choose two children to start as taggers and play the game once without interruption. Only intervene to clarify rules if needed.

Adaptations

↓ You could allow children to decide to start the game with two tails if they want a bit of support.

↓ You could add in some safe zones where children can stay for up to ten seconds without being tagged.

Assessment for learning

Tag games provide us with lots of opportunities to explore and discuss tactics and decisions. In this game, the taggers are the defenders. They are defenders because they are trying to stop and block the others from moving.

● Why is it more difficult to escape when there are more taggers?

● If you are trying to escape from the taggers, is it easier in a big space or a small space?

● How can two taggers work cleverly to trap those who are trying to escape? Where in the area is this most successful? (Answer: in the corner areas.)

The 'tail' is a bib tucked into the child's waistband or pocket.

Top TIP

Link this game to the class theme. For example, you are Egyptian warriors escaping the griffin, or you are healthy blood cells fleeing from an infection.

Breakout

Pairs of children defend a target, seeking the chance to steal the ball and break out!

How to facilitate the game

1 Show the area. The game takes place in a triangle or square shape, with small cones in each corner. In the middle is a target cone.

2 Demonstrate the game. Three or four children will be the attacking team. They move around on the outside of the shape and can throw and catch the ball between them. Two defenders guard the target cone.

3 Add scoring. Explain the scoring system:

- The attackers need to try to throw the ball so it hits the target cone and they get three points if they can do this.

- They also get one point if they can throw the ball between the two defenders to a teammate.

- The defenders can score five points if they can intercept a pass and run out of the area with the ball without being tagged on their way.

4 Play. Let the children set up their areas and explore the game. Change defenders every so often.

Adaptations

↑ For children who come alive when playing football, the game could be played as a football game with the ball on the floor.

Assessment for learning

The defenders in this game have a dilemma: if they leave the target to try to intercept the ball, the target is open and vulnerable to attack. The defenders also need to maintain a close distance to each other, otherwise they give away points by allowing passes between them.

These questions should be asked once all children have had the chance to be a defender in the game.

- Why do you need to stay close to each other when you defend in this game?

- When might be a good chance to intercept a pass between attackers?

- If one defender goes to try to intercept a pass, what is the role of the other defender?

Pitch with a goal or targets

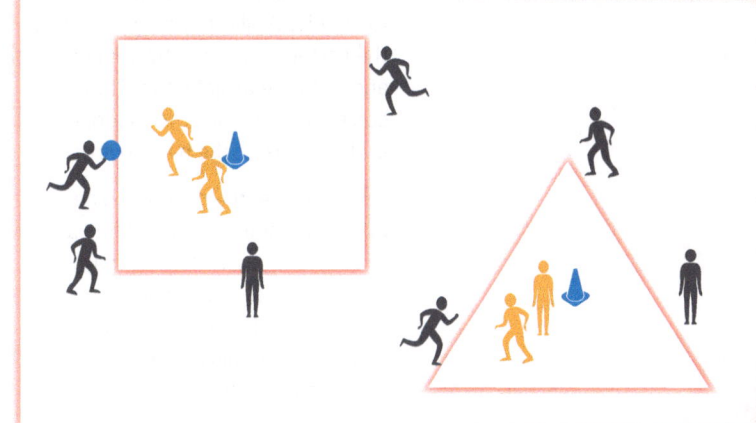

Aim
To defend as a pair, practising intercepting and covering.

Set-up

Grouping:
Groups of six.

Equipment needed:
Each game will need three or four small cones, one large target cone and a ball.

Space needed:
Each game takes place on a small court.

143

Aim

To defend spaces and to work as a team to retrieve the balls quickly.

Set-up

Grouping:
Teams of four.

Equipment needed:
For each game you will need four hoops, four small cones and four tennis balls.

Space needed:
Each game takes place on a small court. (See diagram on page xvii.)

Field of dreams

A small-sided, high-activity striking and fielding game.

How to facilitate the game

1 Show the area. The batting team will need four hoops set up near each other in the middle of the court. These hoops are the batting areas, from which the ball will be struck into the field. A few metres from each batting area, place a small target cone.

2 Demonstrate the game. Four children will need to come and be the batting team. They will each go and stand at a hoop with a tennis ball. Four other children will be the defending team. The batting team will all strike their balls at the same time. They will do this by bouncing the ball in the hoop and striking it with the palm of the hand when it rises after one bounce. The defending team needs to retrieve all four balls and return them to the batting area. They are allowed to run with the ball in their hands in order to do this. While they are doing this, the batters can score by running to and from the target cone. They can keep their collective score on a whiteboard at the batting area.

3 Play. Ask the children to get into teams of four and find a team to play against. They may need help with this. If you have table groups for numeracy or literacy, you could use those groups to form teams or games.

Adaptations

↑ For older classes, the children could use a bat to strike the ball. A noodle is a good bat in this context because it is soft.

↑ You can progress this game by adding the rule that defenders can get the batter 'out' if they catch the ball before it bounces, or if they get the ball to the target cone or batting area before the batter gets there. This would mean the batter's score doesn't count for that hit (the batter isn't actually out of the game).

Assessment for learning

Our questioning will focus on improving the understanding of the four players who are defending the area. In this game, the defenders should gain an understanding of each batter's competence and ability and adjust their starting position accordingly. The defenders might be able to work out that the likely path of the ball will depend on the batter's body position and which hand they use to bat.

● How do you decide where to stand before the batter has hit the ball?

● What can you learn about the batter which will help you defend better?

● How might you work as a team to defend more effectively?

● In which sports might you use the skills we have practised in this game?

The constraints-led approach

The constraints-led approach (CLA) is a way to present learning through games, where the limits, rules and design (the constraints) of the game present learners with specific problems to solve. Learning happens through the players' interactions with the game, manipulated by the constraints on the players, the environment or the task. A well-designed game can therefore quickly lead to the exploration of specific learning intentions and any teaching can be focused directly on these intentions.

Why?

The CLA offers a way of designing and delivering games-based activities that are learner-centred and allow for lots of game play (games and play being optimal features of children's interest and motivation).

Using the CLA in PE allows the teacher to consider the unique needs and behaviours of their children and design games or activities that present them with specific problems to explore and contexts to learn from.

What?

The CLA is based on an underlying theoretical framework called ecological dynamics, which is concerned with how an environment and context can affect perceptions and behaviours.

In CLA, the learner is challenged to find their own solution to the movement problems that are presented in the game. The constraints will mean the learner is likely to explore the game in a specific way, so a well-designed game will include constraints that result in repetitions of specific situations or problems.

How?

CLA requires clever and effective game design to produce and adapt games that target specific interactions between the task, environment and players. For example, a teacher who would like their class to explore passing the ball in invasion games may condition their games to reward teams that make more passes. This could be done through changing the scoring system so that a goal scored after more than three passes is worth double. This change in task will mean that players interact with the game in a different way, with a greater value now given to a pass in the build-up to a goal.

See Press or Drop? (page 146) for an example of the CLA in action.

In Field of Dreams, we use a constraint to encourage throwing and catching: the defenders (the fielders) are not allowed to move if they have the ball. With this added constraint, they will discover that they need to work together to get the ball back to the batting tee.

More information

● Renshaw, I. and Chow, J. Y. (2018), 'A constraint-led approach to sport and physical education pedagogy', *Physical Education and Sport Pedagogy*, 24, (2), 103–116.

Aim

To explore the defensive tactics of pressing the ball or dropping into a compact shape.

Set-up

Grouping:
Teams of four or five.

Equipment needed:
Each game will need one ball, two goals and a centre line.

Space needed:
Each pitch hosts two teams. A large pitch is needed for each game (a netball court size is ideal). See diagram on page xvii.

Press or drop?

A small-sided Key Stage 2 game that uses the constraints-led approach to explore defensive principles and strategy.

How to facilitate the game

1 Set up the pitches. The pitches need to be large so we can explore defending principles in detail. If the pitches are too small then defending becomes too easy. Each pitch needs a centre line, which could be a line on the floor of the playground or denoted by floor spots. Each pitch needs a goal at each end. This could be two cones separated by three metres.

2 Add scoring. The main constraint to this game is the scoring system, which is designed to ensure certain defensive principles are explored. Explain to the children they are going to play a game of football but that there are special instructions about what each goal is worth. Provide each team of children with one of the following instructions:

- Team A: If you win the ball back in the opposition half of the pitch and then go and score, this goal is worth ten points.

- Team B: If you win the ball back in your half of the pitch and then go and score, this goal is worth ten points.

3 Encourage team talk. Provide each team with some time to discuss their approach to the game. Focus on the following questions:

- How will you defend?

- What will you do when your team loses the ball?

- How will you remind each other of your strategy?

4 Play. Let the children play. You may need to check they have understood the scoring system correctly and remind them of how they score the most points. (Note: this game could also be played as a basketball game or a hockey game.)

Assessment for learning

Tactically, this is probably the most complex game in the book for teachers to deliver and for children to understand and succeed in. The instructions given to the teams require them to defend in a particular way in order to score more points. So, each team will either need to:

- drop into a compact defensive shape to protect their goal and win the ball back in their own half; or

- put pressure on the ball and win the ball in the opponents' half of the pitch.

The first question below checks for understanding of the task, then the later questions seek to explore how to implement the different tactics.

- Where on the pitch do you need to win the ball to score more points? Therefore, what do you need to do as soon as your team loses the ball?

- When does your tactic work best?

- What are the key features of a good press? What are the things you need to get right if you drop and defend near your own goal? (See below for some possible answers to these questions.)

- Why might we decide to use a pressing tactic in a game? When might we decide to drop and defend near our own goal?

Key features of a good 'press' when defending

- Pressure is applied at a time when the ball can't easily be played forward. This could be when the opponents have passed the ball slowly or miscontrolled the ball, or when they are facing their own goal with the ball.

- Pressure is applied quickly by two or more defenders working together.

- The collective pressure traps the ball into an area of the pitch.

- Teammates are ready to intercept any passes.

Key features of successful 'dropping' when defending

- Everyone (or almost everyone) on the team has 'dropped' back into the space between the ball and the goal they are defending.

- Someone is putting pressure on the ball in order to stop a shot at goal or a direct forward pass.

- Teammates are positioned in a small shape so the ball cannot be passed between them.

- Teammates are aware of where attacking players are and are ready to intercept any passes.

- When the ball is passed between the attackers, all the defenders quickly move to respond to the new situation. (They move as the ball moves rather than wait for it to arrive.)

Classroom debate

When defending, is it more important to be fast or clever?

The white team makes a diamond shape to try to defend and win the ball back in their own half. This shape makes it hard for the orange team to get to their goal. The nearest white team player to the ball puts pressure on the ball and tries to win it back. The other white team defenders mark opponents and cover spaces nearer the goal.

April

Attacking skills

National Curriculum links

KS1:
'Pupils should be taught to develop **simple tactics** for attacking.'

KS2:
'Pupils should be taught to apply **basic principles** suitable for attacking.'

Key skills

Simple tactics for attacking (KS1)

Move to

- attack the spaces where there are fewest defenders

- catch defenders off-guard (with quick, creative and disguised movements)

- get past defenders while they are distracted (in invasion games only)

Basic principles suitable for attacking (KS2)

Move to

- make spaces between and around opponents

- spread out and use more of the area

- keep the ball, play forward when possible, and try to score (in invasion games only)

An introduction to attacking skills

In many ways, attacking is the opposite of defending. When defending, we are trying to deny and reduce space, and when attacking, we are trying to create and utilise it. Attacking is generally more popular with children, as it allows for a greater degree of surprise and disguise – and scoring goals or points, of course. This month, we will continue looking at 'tactics' and 'principles' through a variety of games that will help broker key discussions and explorations on attacking.

In Four Square Pairs (page 160), which is a 'net or wall' game, we explore how a pair of attackers might work together to create a chance to score.

In The Empire Strikes Back (page 166), which is a 'striking and fielding' game, we explore where we might send objects in order to maximise the amount of time it takes for fielders to retrieve them.

In Capture the Flag (page 161), which is an 'invasion' game, we explore how our collective movements as a team can produce spaces between defenders and create pathways for teammates to move through safely.

In 2v2 Cone Ball (page 158), we use pairs instead of large-sided teams so that all children get more time to practise attacking with the ball.

Invasion games: technical and tactical interventions to teach attacking skills

There are many teaching techniques you could use to make interventions in PE, either to intervene to teach an individual child or to intervene with a small group or whole class. Five types of intervention are included in the matrix below, with examples provided for simple attacking tactics (KS1) and more complex ideas concerning basic attacking principles (KS2).

We want primary school children to become comfortable and confident with the ball in invasion games. The term 'staying on the ball' refers to their ability to control the ball, protect the ball and use the ball purposefully, rather than just kick or throw the ball as soon as they receive it. The interventions in the matrix provide examples of how we might help children develop the skills of 'staying on the ball'.

	KS1: Simple attacking tactics		KS2: Basic attacking principles
TRIAL AND ERROR	Try to take your first touch away from your opponent(s).	Try to bend knees and stay low when you are shielding the ball.	Try to decide how to support your teammate before they receive the ball.
COMMAND	I want you to receive the ball so your opponent can't reach and get it.	Demand the ball more often so your teammates know you are ready.	When your teammate needs support, move to a place where they can see your feet.
GUIDED DISCOVERY	Show me how to use your body to protect the ball.	Show me that you know when the best time is to release the ball.	Show me how to react positively when your teammate wins the ball.
OBSERVATION AND FEEDBACK	Watch how Kyri changes direction to get past the defender.	Watch how Hannah moves towards the ball to stop the defender from intercepting.	Count how many times Khadija receives the ball in free space.
QUESTION AND ANSWER	How might a quick change of speed help you to get past the defender?	What could you do with your body to make the defender think you're going to the left?	What is stopping you from playing a forward pass? How do you know?

A 1v1 version of Pirate Attack (page 212). When are you attacking and when are you defending?

Attacking: individual challenges for invasion games

When it comes to understanding and applying attacking skills in games there will likely be a wide variety of abilities within your class. One way to deal with this is to consider providing individual children with specific challenges. Some individual challenges might be simple and straightforward and help children who are struggling to focus on one key aspect of attacking. Other challenges might be more complex and engage talented attackers with a focused, higher-level challenge.

These challenges can be given to children in games. You can do this in a variety of ways:

- You could call someone over while the game is going on and give them a challenge before sending them back in to see if they can fulfil it.

- You can make challenge cards for attacking (to keep in your PE cupboard). Hand these out to individuals or teams during games.

- You could have a whiteboard with the challenges written on and children can come over and choose which to attempt next.

The challenges

Try to...

- change direction quickly to beat an opponent

- use your weaker foot or hand to receive and pass the ball

- start and stop suddenly to lose your opponent

- dribble (or move with the ball) between two opponents

- make quick, early passes to keep the ball moving

- start a passing move by passing to a teammate and moving forward into a new space afterwards

- pass the ball forward quickly and early when you can

- always be in a position to receive a pass from a teammate

- remain calm when you have the ball

- decide what to do with the ball before the ball gets to you

- keep possession of the ball by playing the ball backwards when you can't go forwards

- set up someone else to score a goal

- as a goalkeeper, dribble out of goal and start an attack

- as a goalkeeper, always be available to receive a pass from a teammate who has no one to pass to.

Tag games are a good way to begin teaching attacking skills. The attackers in a tag game are the ones trying to escape from the taggers. They need to consider moving into spaces and changing direction to dodge and escape.

Key vocabulary for attacking in invasion games

- **Assist:** To pass to a teammate who then scores a goal or point.
- **Early pass:** To pass soon after you have received the ball.
- **First touch:** Your first touch of the ball when you receive a pass from a teammate.
- **Intercept:** To steal the ball while it is being passed between attackers.
- **Keep possession:** Dribble or pass by yourself or with teammates so the opposition don't get the ball.

- **Pass forward:** A pass that moves the ball closer to the goal you are trying to score in.
- **Receive the ball:** To catch a throw or control a pass.
- **Release the ball:** To send the ball by passing or shooting it.
- **Shielding:** Protecting the ball using your body; your body is a shield with the ball on one side and the opponent on the other.
- **Support:** To move to a position where a teammate who has the ball can pass to you.

Skittle fall

Fool your partner to knock down their skittle.

Aim

To pretend to be aiming one way, but change and shoot the other way instead (to disguise intentions).

Set-up

Grouping:
Pairs.

Equipment needed:
Four skittles (or other objects) plus at least one beanbag or tennis ball per pair.

Space needed:
Any.

How to facilitate the game

1 Demonstrate the game. Ask two children to demonstrate. They kneel opposite each other, a few metres apart. To the left and right of each of them is a skittle. They take it in turns to slide a beanbag (or roll a tennis ball) along the floor, attempting to knock down one of their opponent's skittles. Children can try to stop the beanbag from hitting the skittle by intercepting the beanbag before it reaches the skittle.

2 Play. The children can organise their own games. You may need to go around and check distances are realistic, so the children are not too far from each other, and the skittles are not too far from nor too close to each child.

Adaptations

This game could become dull before long, so here are two ways to liven it up.

↓ The skittles could be moved further away from each other after each unsuccessful attempt. This allows the game to be made easier for children who are not experiencing success.

↑ If you have enough beanbags, you could provide each pair with two of them. The thrower then has two attempts instead of one. This gives them the chance to move the defender one way with their first slide, and then aim towards the opposite side for the second slide.

Assessment for learning

This game provides the opportunity to consider the attacking tactic of fooling an opponent through pretence and disguise. The questions below probe this area of attacking, although it may be worth showing the class what good disguise looks like through a demonstration.

● What signals do you give that tell your partner which skittle you are aiming for? (Answer: aiming, looking, position of your hips and shoulders.)

● How might changing the speed of your delivery help to launch a surprise attack? (Answer: the opponent is not ready to defend.)

Top TIP

This game could be adapted for wheelchair users by asking the children to throw the beanbag or tennis ball while seated in a chair instead of kneeling.

Noodle tag

A pairs tag battle involving quick reactions and clever movements.

How to facilitate the game

1 Show the area. This game has boundaries, with each end of the playing area being a safe area that players are trying to run to.

2 Demonstrate the game. Demonstrate the game with a pair of children. The pair of children stand facing each other in the middle of the playing area. There is a noodle (or scarf or bib) on the floor between them. They play a game of rock, paper, scissors, with the winner immediately running away, and the loser grabbing the noodle to chase them. The chaser should try to tag the runner with the noodle before they reach the end of the playing area.

3 Play. The children can find their own partner, get their own noodle and begin playing. It is important that all pairs start their activity next to each other so that all the racing and chasing happens parallel to each other and collisions are avoided.

Adaptations

Switch partners. You may get uneven matches between fast and slow children in this activity. One way of dealing with this is to switch partners after every three or four turns. Another way is to slow down the faster runners by challenging them to hop for double points, or to bounce a ball as they move.

↑ To begin with, the child who runs to escape can get one point for making it safely to the end of the playing area. You can then progress to awarding three points if the player runs away but then turns, gets past their opponent with the noodle, and makes it to their opponent's end of the playing area.

Assessment for learning

In this game, the winner of the rock, paper, scissors contest becomes the attacker and they must run away to escape the defender who chases them. However, this may not be obvious to the children, so we explore this in the first two questions below. The final question reflects on the skills needed to double back and beat the defender once you add the 'three points' progression.

● What skills do you need to escape from your opponent when you win the game of rock, paper, scissors?

● Are you a defender or an attacker when you are escaping? What is the difference?

● What do you need to do well in order to get three points in this game?

Aim

To move quickly to escape and outrun a defender.

Set-up

Grouping:
Pairs.

Equipment needed:
One noodle per pair (or a scarf or bib). Lines or spots on the floor to denote the safe areas.

Space needed:
Any.

⊚ Aim

To use your body to protect the ball.

✚ Set-up

Grouping:
Pairs.

Equipment needed:
One bib and
one ball per pair.

Space needed:
Any.

Lots of pairs can share the same small area. This forces the children to look around them all the time and make decisions continually about where and how to move.

Bib v ball

Children throw the bib so it hits the ball in this one-against-one battle.

How to facilitate the game

1 Demonstrate the game.
You will need two children to demonstrate. One child has a bib and one child has a ball. The child with the ball can choose how they move with the ball. They might throw and catch it, bounce it or dribble it with their hands or feet. The child with the bib needs to throw the bib so it touches the ball. The child with the ball needs to protect the ball to stop the bib from touching it. After three bib throws, the children change roles.

2 Play. The children can find their own partner and equipment. To begin with, allow them to play within a large square area. All the pairs play at once, all sharing the same space. After a couple of goes each, restrict the child with the ball to either bouncing the ball or dribbling it with the feet.

Adaptations

↑ You could consider reducing the space so the child with the ball can't run away. This forces them to find other ways of protecting the ball, such as using their body to protect it.

↑ You could also progress this activity by adding direction: mark out two large rectangles on the floor and challenge the child with the ball to get from one rectangle to another without letting the bib hit the ball.

↑ For older classes, this game could be progressed to a 2v2 game with one pair with a ball against another pair with a bib. In this version, the pairs can pass the ball or bib between them. If you do this, then restrict the size of the area that the game is played in so the attacking tactics can be explored.

Assessment for learning

This game is interesting because both roles involve elements of attacking and defending. The child with the bib is attacking when they throw the bib to try to hit the ball. The child with the ball is attacking when they try to use the space to protect the ball. You could therefore focus your questions on either role.

● Bib: What stops you from making a successful throw? How do you move your opponent so you can see the ball and make a successful throw?

● Ball: How do you use your body to protect the ball from your opponent?

Top TIP
Be careful about playing this game in a place with a smooth or slippery floor surface. Bibs are likely to be thrown near the children's feet as they move and this is a safety hazard.

Spike ball

A quick-reaction competitive ball game with a focus on clever attacking skills.

How to facilitate the game

1 Demonstrate the game. Make a small square shape on the floor using spots. Ask four children to come out and demonstrate the game. One child should stand on each side of the square. Each game has a ball, and the ball is bounced into the square by each child, with the aim of sending the ball towards another child on a different side of the square. To begin with, challenge the children to work together to get a successful rally of eight passes without a mistake.

2 Play. The children find groups of four, make their square shape and begin. If your class size is not divisible by four, groups of three can play around a triangle in exactly the same way.

3 Make it competitive. In order to teach attacking skills, this game needs to become competitive. In the competitive version of this game, each child protects their side of the square, and tries to score by bouncing the ball past children on the other sides. Each child starts with five lives. They lose a life if the ball bounces in the square, crosses their side of the square and they don't manage to catch it or return it.

Adaptations

↓ Some children may need to catch the ball and throw it back into the square rather than pat it with their hands.

↑ For higher-ability children, this game could be played by patting or striking the ball with the palm of the hand. You could even add a racket or bat for some children to use.

Assessment for learning

In net and wall and striking and fielding games, a simple attacking tactic is to try to send the ball into the spaces where it is hardest for your opponent(s) to reach. In order to do this well, children will need to look at their opponents regularly to recognise where the gaps are between them.

● When is it hardest to return the ball? OR: Where is the best place to send the ball if you want to get it past your opponent?

● How do you know where to send the ball?

Aim

To send the ball into the spaces away from your opponents.

Set-up

Grouping:
Groups of four.

Equipment needed:
Each group will need four floor spots and one bouncy ball.

Space needed:
Any.

Cross-curricular link

Instead of starting with five lives, you could have children practise their times tables by starting with a much higher number and subtracting larger amounts. For example, the children start with 70 lives and subtract seven lives each time they lose.

Aim

To move to support your teammate when attacking.

Set-up

Grouping:
Pairs.

Equipment needed:
Each game will need one tall cone and one ball.

Space needed:
Each game takes place between two pairs. There are no boundaries to pitches so all games are played in overlapping areas. This will therefore work in a small space.

2v2 cone ball

A two-a-side invasion game with a tall cone as a goal.

How to facilitate the game

1 Demonstrate the game. This game could be played in any invasion game format but works really well as football, basketball or hockey. Place a cone in the middle of the area. Get four children to demonstrate and put them into two teams of two children each. The two teams play against each other, with both teams needing to hit the ball against the tall cone to score.

2 Play. Ask the children to find pairs and groups of four and begin to play.

Adaptations

Children who are more able in the invasion game you are playing will have an advantage and may need a challenge, while others may struggle and need support. Alternatively (or additionally), you can observe the games and switch some teams around to make more even contests.

↓ Adapt the rules so children can have two free bounces (in basketball) or two free touches (in football) when they get the ball. They can't be tackled during these bounces or touches.

↑ Challenge children to see if they can set up their teammate to score (you could offer half a point if they make an assist). Or, see if they can play with just passes and no dribbling, so they rely on their teammates.

Assessment for learning

This game is perfect for starting to explore the basic principles of movement and support when attacking. We focus our teaching on the teammate of the player who has the ball. Their role is to get into a position where they can receive a pass, ideally nearer to the cone than their teammate with the ball.

● How do you know where to move so you can support your teammate?

● What might you do if an opponent follows you when you move?

● Where is the best place to receive a pass from your teammate?

See page 148 for a photo of this game in action with a KS2 class.

Follow the leader

Children work together in pairs in this instant-start activity.

How to facilitate the game

1 Explain the game. Tell the children they are going to play a game of 'follow the leader'. Both the leader and follower have a ball each and they can decide how they move with their ball. The follower will need to follow and copy everything the leader does. Challenge the leader to lose their follower.

2 Play. 'Find a partner and off you go!' If you have an odd number, have a group of three with one leader and two followers.

3 Add obstacles. Obstacles like benches and hula hoops may encourage a wider exploration of movements. You can add these additions while the children are having their first turn at the game. Put in some 'gates' on the floor with pairs of coloured spots about a metre apart.

4 Switch partners. This is a useful way to keep the activity interesting and to spread movement ideas around to different children. Simply stop the activity and say, 'Find a new partner and play again!' There is no need to bring all the children over to you in order to do this.

Adaptations

↑ To add competition and scoring, challenge the follower to see if they can catch the leader by tagging them. The follower could get a point by catching up with the leader and hitting the leader's ball with their own.

Assessment for learning

In this game, we will work with the leader. They are the attacker as they need to try to lose the follower. They can do this by using simple tactics of changing speed and direction. Children may also use the tactic of disguising their intentions by pretending to go one way but then suddenly moving in a different direction.

● How might you move so you lose your follower? What tactics have worked for you?

● Who is really hard to follow? What do they do well? (Possible answers: sudden movements, changing direction and speed at the same time, pretending to go one way but then going in a different direction.)

Set-up

Grouping:
Pairs.

Equipment needed:
An assortment of balls or objects to travel with, and cones, spots, benches, hoops or other obstacles for the floor.

Space needed:
Any.

Can the leader use changes of speed and direction to lose their follower?

Four square pairs

A four-player tennis game in small squares.

How to facilitate the game

1 Demonstrate the game. Each court is a square, made up of four smaller squares. You will need four children to demonstrate, with each child assigned to one of the smaller squares. The game is played by bouncing the ball into each other's squares, using the palm of the hand. The ball is allowed to bounce once in each square before being returned to a different square. Ask the four children to demonstrate what this looks like for the rest of the class to observe.

2 Add scoring. If a player hits the ball into another square and the ball bounces twice in that square, they score a point.

If a player hits the ball into another square and it bounces once and is not returned to another square by the opponent, they score a point.

3 Play. Children can find their own groups and put together their own areas using floor spots.

4 Switch to 2v2. Bring the children in and explain the following progression: the game will now be played as a 2v2 game, with the two players diagonally opposite each other on the same team.

Adaptations

↓ You can change the size of some of the squares, so someone who is struggling could have a smaller square.

↓ Younger children could throw and catch the ball instead of patting it back with their palm.

↑ You could add rackets for those children who are finding things easy.

Assessment for learning

This game builds on the attacking concepts taught in Spike Ball (page 157). In Four Square Pairs, we start to consider how we set up (or assist) our teammate to score a point. The 2v2 version of the game allows pairs of children to work together to provide each other with a pass that is easy to use to attack an opponent's square.

● When is it best to try to score and when is it best to pass to your teammate?

● What kind of pass do you want from your teammate so you can score?

● How is working together in PE similar to working together in numeracy or literacy?

Capture the flag

Teams must work together to invade an area and steal treasure.

How to facilitate the game

1 Show the court. Each game will take place between two teams on a small court. Each court has a half-way line and five pieces of treasure at each end. You could show this on a whiteboard, as well as in reality. It may be a good idea to set up the courts while the children are engaged in a quick starter game.

2 Explain the game. Each team defends one end of the court. They aim to invade the opponents' half, steal a piece of treasure and return it to their own end. After a player has crossed the half-way line and entered the opponents' half, they can be tagged. If they are tagged, they must return to their own treasure area and re-join the game from there. A player cannot be tagged when returning with a piece of treasure. The winning team is the team that gets all pieces of treasure to their end.

3 Play. Children may need help getting into teams efficiently (see page 39).

Adaptations

↓ The amount of success in the game will depend largely on the size of the court. A bigger area is harder to defend, so the children will capture pieces of treasure more regularly. If you can only make small courts due to space restrictions, consider a rule that children can only be tagged on their back. This will make it easier for them to enter the opponents' half without getting caught.

↑ For older classes, or for children who are confident with a ball, you could give each team a ball to dribble with. Instead of getting tagged, the player with a ball is caught if an opponent touches the ball.

Assessment for learning

Success in this game happens when a team's collective movements open up spaces in the opponents' half for someone to get through. Often an adventure across the half-way line may end up with a child being tagged, but their movement may still have been very valuable if they got an opponent out of the way to create a pathway for a teammate. Movement to create space for others is a basic principle of attacking in invasion games.

● How might you move into the opponents' half so you create space for a teammate? How might you sacrifice yourself in order to help a teammate succeed?

● How might you coordinate your movements as a team to help one of you get across safely?

Classroom debate

'If you are a good attacker in basketball, you are likely to also be a good attacker in hockey, tennis and cricket.' Discuss.

Aim

To move to create space for a teammate.

Set-up

Grouping:
Teams of four or five.

Equipment needed:
Each game will need ten cones or beanbags as treasure to steal, plus something to mark the half-way line on pitches (e.g. a chalk line or floor spots).

Space needed:
Each game will be played on a small court. See the diagram on page xvii.

Aim

To spread out
and to move and
support each other
as a team.

Set-up

Grouping:
Teams of four to five.

Equipment needed:
Each pitch will need
an end zone marked
out with cones or
lines on the floor.

Space needed:
Each pitch hosts
two teams, competing
together. You'll need
three pitches for a class
of 30. See the diagram
on page xvii for
pitch set-up.

Invisiball

*A small-sided Key Stage 2 invasion game
where the ball is invisible.*

How to facilitate the game

1 Show the pitch. The game is played between two teams of four or five children each. Each pitch has an end zone at each end. To score, players need to run with the ball into the end zone or catch the ball in the end zone.

2 Explain the game. There is no ball! Here are the rules:

● There is only an imaginary ball and children represent being in possession of the ball by placing their hand flat on the top of their head.

● A child in possession of the 'ball' can move with the ball as long as they move with their hand on their head.

● If the child in possession of the 'ball' is tagged by an opponent, then possession is lost. The tagged child takes their hand off their head and the opponent who tagged them places their hand on their own head, signifying a change in possession.

● Children can pass the 'ball' to any of their teammates at any point by pointing to their teammate and saying their name loudly. When a pass is made, the passer takes their hand off their head and the receiver puts their hand on their head.

3 Play. This may take a while to get used to. Allow the children some time to play this before trying to teach attacking skills.

Adaptations

↓ A larger pitch will make it easier for the attacking team to keep the ball and make good decisions. If you have enough space, use large pitches rather than small ones.

↑ Children may quickly work out that a good way to score is to put one of their team standing in the end zone and quickly pass to that player. To respond, add this rule: you can only score by running into the end zone, not by receiving a pass in the end zone; and you cannot spend more than three seconds within two metres of the end zone.

Assessment for learning

This is a wonderful game once the children get used to how it works. To be successful, they will need to make quick and early decisions about moving and passing. The attacking team really needs to spread out and use all the space in order to move the imaginary ball around safely and look for opportunities to pass forward. The first question below considers individual players' decision-making about moving or passing. The second and third questions explore moving forward to score.

● When are you able to attack by moving forward? When may you need to pass the ball?

162

- What might happen to the spaces between the defenders when you spread out and pass the 'ball' around? (Answer: the spaces might get bigger as the defenders are moved around and this may present an opportunity to play forward safely.)

- When is a good time to quickly and suddenly attack? (Answer: when your team has just won the ball because the opponents may not be ready to defend.)

Top TIP

There will likely be some disputes as the children learn this game. It is quite common for more than one child to be running around with their hand on their head, so it can be unclear who has the ball in this game. It may be worth revisiting some of the fair play and resolving disputes advice from September (page 21).

163

Teaching Games for Understanding

Teaching Games for Understanding (TGfU) is a model for teaching and learning where learning happens through a modified game that poses tactical problems for learners to solve. The game is taught first before game understanding is enhanced through a collaborative inquiry into tactical decisions. The aim of this approach is to enhance the understanding of games like the one being played, and to identify and refine the key skills needed to be successful.

Why?

Traditional models for PE involve the teaching of techniques out of context and in isolation to the game within which they are required. Consider two children throwing and catching a ball between them at basketball practice. They might get better at throwing and catching, but there may be limited transfer of these techniques once they are put into a game context. The isolated throwing and catching practice has not helped them understand the tactics needed in basketball.

A TGfU approach recognises that techniques, skills and understanding might be best developed through game play. It appreciates that games can be grouped into categories (e.g. invasion games) and that the principles and strategies required are the same or similar for all games within each group. So, a development of understanding in tactics and principles in a modified basketball game may provide relevant learning that can be applied to all types of invasion game. Importantly, the process of learning through play and games is a better fit for children in primary school than boring and repetitive technical 'work'.

What?

TGfU starts with the game (or a modified version of it), and activities begin with a focus on playing and understanding the game. As the children play, they begin to understand the key rules that shape the game and the tactics needed to be successful. This understanding can be shared through questioning and dialogue. Learners in a TGfU lesson will develop an appreciation of the influence of space, time and movement on their decision-making, and improve their understanding of when, why and how to execute the key skills needed in the game. As confidence and understanding grow, the learners move towards better performance of the game.

How?

You will need to design a game that allows everyone to be involved. Typically, this means that team size will be reduced so that all children can experience repetitive episodes of decision-making within the game context. For primary school PE, it should be a simple game that is easily explained and that the children can explore by themselves with limited intervention.

The teachers' role is to observe how the children explore the game, and to decide when and how to intervene to share knowledge among the children. As mentioned, in TGfU, learning and understanding are shared through questioning and dialogue. The teacher should lead these interventions with well-planned, open questions. All children should be involved in discussing and answering them.

See The Empire Strikes Back (page 166) for an example of the TGfU model in action.

More information

- Stolz, S. and Pill, S. (2013), 'Teaching games and sport for understanding: Exploring and reconsidering its relevance in physical education', *European Physical Education Review*, 20, (1), 36–71.
- Visit playsport.net for some TGfU activities.

Use the TGfU method
to teach Pirate Attack
(page 212). Allow the
children to explore the
game first before asking
them questions that help
share and develop their
understanding of roles
and tactics.

Aim

To explore where and how to send objects so they are hardest for the fielders to return.

Set-up

Grouping:
Groups of four or five.

Equipment needed:
Each game will need three tennis balls, three cones, one hoop, and a mini whiteboard to keep score.

Space needed:
Small courts will work well. See the diagram on page xvii.

The empire strikes back

A striking and fielding game using the Teaching Games for Understanding (TGfU) method.

How to facilitate the game

1 Show the court. Each court has a starting area (the hoop) and three bases (the cones). The three bases together with the hoop make a small diamond shape.

2 Explain the game. Children take turns to be Darth Vader.

● The first Vader starts in the hoop and rolls three Death Stars (the tennis balls) forward into the court.

● As soon as they have rolled the third and final Death Star, the Rebel team (the fielding team) must rush to return the Death Stars to the hoop.

● While they are doing that, Darth Vader can score a point by running around the three bases before all Death Stars are returned to the hoop.

● Darth Vader then adds their score to the whiteboard and swaps with one of the Rebel team.

3 Play. Children can find their own groups and set up their own areas.

Adaptations

↓ Additional targets could be added to the fielding area. Darth Vader can freeze the Rebels for five seconds if able to send a Death Star so it hits one of these additional targets.

↓ Darth Vader positions each member of the Rebel team (telling them where to stand) before rolling the Death Stars.

Assessment for learning using a TGfU approach

To begin with, children explore the game by playing it. Our questions intend to aid children's understanding of the game. In this game, Darth Vader is the attacker. We need to focus on their decisions about where to send the three Death Stars.

Depending on what you observe, here are some questions that could get the children thinking about where and how they send the Death Stars into the fielding area.

● What are you trying to achieve when you roll the three Death Stars?

● Which kinds or rolls have been most difficult for the fielders to return?

● Is it better to roll for distance or for accuracy?

● How does the position of the Rebels affect where you roll the Death Stars? What else do you need to consider when you roll the Death Stars?

Many of the games in this book are set up to be taught using a TGfU approach, with children experiencing a modified game and questions designed to aid understanding of it and link learning to other similar games.

Six small games of The Empire Strikes Back on a netball court. There is more involvement and learning per child in this set-up than if you play a whole-class game with large teams.

 Cross-curricular link

Instead of Death Stars, you could name the tennis balls after real planets. For younger children, this could act as a review of the planet names. For older children, you could challenge the children to roll the planets in order of their distance from the Sun.

167

Meaningful experiences in PE: guiding principles

In order to be impactful and to positively shape future lives, education experiences should resonate with children in some way. Children will find personal significance in activities and experiences for a variety of reasons. Importantly, these reasons may be different from our own reasons to move, play or compete. The most common reasons are summed up in the themes presented in the table below, reproduced with permission from Alex Beckey's blog post on meaningful experiences in PE (available at: https://drowningintheshallow.wordpress.com).

You might find the 'belief into action statements' a useful framework to consider and compare against your own beliefs. If you want to create more meaningful PE experiences for your children, these statements could also provide a set of criteria with which to evaluate your delivery of PE.

ELEMENTS	BELIEF INTO ACTION STATEMENTS
MEANINGFUL EXPERIENCES	We believe in creating meaningful experiences within physical education... so we look to prioritise the interplay of fun, social interactions, challenge, motor competence and personally relevant learning... and resist the urge to see them as by-products of participation.
CHALLENGE	We believe that appropriate challenge leads to enjoyment and continued motivation... so we provide experiences that place an emphasis on the challenge inherent in the process of completing the task... and resist the urge to see challenge solely through the binary of winning and losing.
MOTOR COMPETENCE	We believe that developing motor competence is one of the best approaches to develop confidence... so we take a holistic approach to competence... and resist the urge to solve all physical problems with only physical solutions.
FUN	We believe that fun is an essential part of creating meaningful experiences... so we seek to plan for fun by understanding our pupils' culture and community values... and resist the urge to prioritise fun at the expense of other meaningful criteria.
SOCIAL INTERACTION	We believe that positive social interactions are at the heart of meaningful movement experiences in PE... so we seek to carefully consider the way we organise opportunities for social interactions... and resist the urge always to control the relationships within the learning context.
PERSONALLY RELEVANT LEARNING	We believe that experiences in PE can be made more personally relevant... when we help co-create and connect the children's learning to their idea of a 'good life' beyond school... and resist the urge to assume what is important for us is important for them.

More information   For more on meaning in PE, see: Beni, S., Fletcher, T. and Ní Chróinín, D. (2017), 'Meaningful experiences in physical education and youth sport: A review of the literature', *Quest*, 69, (3), 291–312.

Five ways to raise the value and impact of PE in your school

Despite understanding the potential value of PE, many schools do not spend enough time or effort to realise its power. Here are five ways you might raise the value of PE and help the subject to have a bigger impact in your school.

1 Engage the school community

Each school is a unique community. A PE curriculum that is co-created by your children, families, teachers and staff will be one that is supported, celebrated and respected.

- Ask children, families and teachers for their views.
- Establish a PE and sports council of children who meet regularly to discuss and enhance the PE and sport programme.
- Communicate regularly with the community through a PE newsletter.
- Co-create a 'Purpose for PE' document that explains your intentions for the subject.

2 Celebrate school values in PE

PE is the perfect subject to explore values like kindness, resilience or determination. The first two chapters show how PE programmes can be adapted to focus on social and thinking skills.

- Identify key success criteria for your school values (for example, 'What does kindness look like?'). Plan a unit of PE to focus on these skills.

3 Link PE, whole-school interventions and classroom subjects

PE does not happen in a vacuum. Children's PE experiences should link solidly to their other school experiences.

- Help children make connections between PE and non-PE subjects. Talk about PE in the classroom. Talk about the classroom in PE.
- PE assemblies offer classes the chance to present learning from PE units of work.
- Link PE outcomes to whole-school improvement targets.

4 Link PE, playtimes, and extra-curricular sport and competition

When these three strands are connected, there is more chance of children enrolling in after-school sport clubs, and more chance of positive competition experiences.

- If you have taught an activity in PE, offer the same equipment to the children at playtime or lunchtime so they can continue playing.
- Uptake of an after-school sport club may increase if the sport is explored positively in PE.
- Inter-school competitions should focus on activities the children have learnt and practised, perhaps linked to an extra-curricular club.

5 Treat PE with respect

Give PE the same status as other subjects.

- PE should happen regularly. Catch up if you miss a lesson.
- Children should not be taken out of PE for catch-up work in other subjects.
- PE lessons should be observed – with high expectations of teaching and learning, child inclusion and behaviour.
- Regular teacher training should be provided.

Sports days

It is traditional to have a sports day in the summer term in primary schools, so this month is a good time to consider how your event might work. The tips and ideas below should help you plan and deliver an event that is engaging, inclusive and unique.

1 Purpose

Consider the purpose of your sports day. What are you hoping to achieve?

You could link your sports day to your:

- School values: It could be a celebration of cooperation or a theme of determination.
- School PE curriculum: You could focus on attacking and defending skills, which we have worked on recently.
- A finale of an intra-school competition: It could mark the end of a Sport Education block of work (see page 222 for more information).

2 Competition

One of the big decisions about sports day is if and how you will include competition.

Some children will relish competitive small-sided team games, while others may prefer team challenges or the opportunity to beat their own score.

- Aim to include opportunities for everyone (who wants to) to compete at their own level and on their own terms. Consider the needs of all the children, including those who don't want to compete but do want to celebrate movement.
- Consider that scoreboards, stopwatches and tape measures may provide narrow definitions of success. Offer children the chance to succeed in a variety of ways, for example, by being the best teammate or making the most effort.

- Perhaps each class teacher could decide how competitive the event should be based on their own knowledge of their class.
- Some schools divide their children into houses, with houses accumulating points for each activity and an overall winner being announced at the end of the event.

3 Activities

Children will remember the activities and how they made them feel. Consider trying out a few ideas with the children in your planning stage.

- You could use a carousel approach with a variety of different kinds of activity (throwing and catching, running and jumping, attacking and defending).
- Aim for a mix of individual, pair and small-team games, with different ways of scoring, completing or winning.
- It may be a good idea to use games that the children have previously explored in PE (like those in this book!).
- Be creative! You could base the games on a theme, perhaps linked to a major sports event or a favourite book series.
- Consider how much involvement there is for each child – so no long queues or waiting around.
- Children usually love a teachers' tug-of-war or a parents' race or similar.

Remember to consider the needs of SEND children in your planning.

173

Arm tennis

Compete or collaborate in this easy, adaptable version of tennis.

Aim

To compare and reflect on experiences of collaboration and competition.

Set-up

Grouping:
Pairs.

Equipment needed:
One bib and one ball per pair.

Space needed:
Any.

A game can be both collaborative and competitive if a pair or team are working together to beat their own score or achieve a personal best.

How to facilitate the game

1 Demonstrate the game. Ask for a volunteer. Hold one end of a bib each to make a net between you. Demonstrate throwing and catching a ball between you, over the net.

2 Explain the task. Tell the class they are going to invent their own game of arm tennis. They must have a bib as a net and they must use a ball. With their partner, they will need to decide if they want to play collaboratively (to try to achieve something together) or competitively (against each other, winning and losing). Tell them that they can change between collaboration and competition when they want.

3 Play. Children should find their own partner, get a bib and a ball, and start by deciding whether to play collaboratively or competitively.

4 Share ideas. Once the children have had a chance to create their own game, match up three pairs and get them to demonstrate their games and try each other's games.

Assessment for learning

This terrific game has an almost endless variety of adaptations and progressions to explore. With encouragement, children should start bouncing the ball either side of the net or going under the net instead of over it. Some might use their feet, some might choose to use two balls instead of one, and so on.

The questions below could broker deep conversations about feelings and experiences.

- Did you and your partner choose to collaborate or to compete? Why?

- What makes a competitive game enjoyable? (This is particularly useful for children who didn't choose competition, as it helps them consider what needs to be in place in order for them to engage in competition.)

- How do you use the skills of collaboration and competition in other parts of school or in your life outside of school?

Top TIP

To share ideas around the class, you could call four pairs over to you. Ask them to take it in turns to show their game so they all have a chance to play each other's games. Then call a different four pairs over and repeat.

Scoop

One child leads and two children compete in this movement and reaction game.

How to facilitate the game

1 Demonstrate the game. Ask for two children to demonstrate with you. Stand them a couple of metres apart, facing each other, with a cone in between them. Tell them that when you say, 'Scoop!', the first one to grab the cone wins the game. Show them how to bend low and reach in to get the cone, so there is no chance of clashing heads. Demonstrate the game, using a variety of quick movement instructions – like 'Balance on one leg', 'Do three star jumps', '360-degree spin' – then 'Scoop!'

2 Play. Ask the class to find a group of three, with two children playing and one leading the game and calling the instructions. They must swap over regularly so everyone gets a chance to lead.

Adaptations

 When leading the game, encourage the children to be inventive and creative with their instructions. You could even add in some more equipment, like a tennis ball for each of the players, so you can include some throwing, catching or bouncing.

Assessment for learning

Some children will relish leading the game, and others will find it uncomfortable. This is a chance for everyone in the class to have a go at being in charge. Reflecting on this experience might help them gain confidence and understanding to enjoy and thrive in roles with responsibility.

- Did you prefer leading the game or playing the game? Why?

- How does the leader make the game enjoyable and engaging for the players? What other skills does a good leader need to have?

- When can you use these skills outside of PE or outside of school life?

Aim

To experience leading and playing and to reflect on how each role feels.

Set-up

Grouping:
Groups of three.

Equipment needed:
One cone per group.

Space needed:
Any.

Giving children the chance to lead a game provides them with the experience of being in charge, being creative and being important.

Cross-curricular link

A game of Scoop can be played with three cones in the middle instead of one. Use a whiteboard marker to write numbers on the cones. You can then add in numeracy skills by asking the leader to call a number instead of shouting, 'Scoop!' Perhaps the players need to grab two cones that multiply to make the number called. Alternatively, write phonemes on the cones. The leader calls a word and the other two children grab the cone that shows the phoneme in that word.

Snowman

An individual bouncing and catching challenge involving a big ball and a small ball.

How to facilitate the game

1 Get the equipment ready. Every child will need two balls for this activity, so make sure they are easily accessible to avoid a chaotic crowd all trying to access them from the same bag or bucket.

2 Demonstrate the game. Hold a large bouncy football or basketball. Place a soft tennis ball on top of it to make a snowman. Make sure the snowman's head is exactly over the middle of the larger ball. Drop the snowman onto the floor. The snowman's head should bounce high into the air. Catch it as it comes back down.

3 Play. 'Get your equipment and have a go.' The children get a point for each time they can catch the snowman's head. Some children will get the hang of this much more quickly than others. Once a child can do it, ask them to go and help someone else to do it.

Assessment for learning

This is a simple but exciting activity. Use soft tennis balls, if possible, as they can rebound quickly and erratically once the larger ball hits the floor.

The questions below intend to get children thinking and talking about their experience with individual challenges. Using the second question, you may be able to explore resilience and determination.

- Did you enjoy the challenge of working on your own, or do you prefer to work with other people?

- How did it feel if you couldn't make the activity work? How did you deal with these feelings?

- How did it feel to teach someone else and show them how to do it? What makes a good teacher?

Aim

To reflect on the experience of trying to master an individual challenge, and of giving or receiving help from a classmate.

Set-up

Grouping:
Individuals.

Equipment needed:
One large bouncy ball and one soft tennis ball per child.

Space needed:
A playing area with a hard surface (not grass).

Top TIP

If you don't have enough balls for each child to have their own, then have one set between two children. Ask them to take turns to drop the snowman and they can both try to catch the small ball.

Birthdays

A whole-class, cooperative activity finding out about each other's age.

Aim

To work cooperatively as a large group and to reflect on your age in relation to the rest of the class.

Set-up

Grouping:
Whole class together.

Equipment needed:
Four spots or cones.

Space needed:
Any.

How to facilitate the game

1 Set up the area. Use the four spots or cones to mark out a square on the floor.

2 Divide the class into four equal-sized groups. Assign each group to one side of the square.

3 Explain the game. Each group must make a line in age order, along their side of the square, with the oldest child at one end and the youngest child at the other end. The first group to do this successfully wins.

Adaptations

↓ For younger classes, you could use height order instead of age order, or offer some help by showing them where the oldest children (typically those with September birthdays) will be and where the youngest (typically those with August birthdays) will be.

↑ You could use benches instead of lines. Arrange four benches in a square and ask children to stand on the benches. They must then rearrange themselves into the required order without anyone falling off the bench.

Assessment for learning

The game itself may take a while and you might find it interesting to see who takes leadership roles and how the children work together. However, some of the main outcomes are explored in the post-activity reflection.

● How did it feel trying to achieve this task together as a group? Would it have been easier or more difficult with a larger group?

For older classes, the following discussions could be interesting ways of exploring age, development and feelings.

● Looking at the other lines, is there a relationship between age and height? Why or why not?

● What is the difference in age between the youngest person in your line and the oldest? What is it like being the oldest or youngest in a group?

Alphabet soup

Small groups use their bodies to create letters on the floor.

How to facilitate the game

1 Demonstrate the game. Ask for five volunteers and arrange the rest of the class so they can see them easily. Ask the volunteers to work together to use their bodies to make the letter T on the floor.

2 Play. Divide the class into groups of four or five and assign each group to an area. Start with some easy letters like O, N and W. Later, add challenge with some trickier letters like S, R or B. Award a point for the quickest team to form the letter and/or the team with the clearest letter. Use a time limit if you want to speed things up.

Adaptations

 You could challenge groups who are performing well by asking them to play silently with no speaking at all. You could assign one person in the group who is the only one who can talk.

Assessment for learning

This activity can be quite challenging as children will have different ideas about how to form the letters. Some children may feel frustrated that others aren't listening to their ideas. Children may need to compromise or find ways of taking it in turns to lead. It may be a good idea to group all the 'leaders' together in one team so you amplify this challenge and force them to deal with having many ideas at once. Other children may not offer any ideas at all and be perfectly happy to be completely led by others. You could group all the quieter children together, as this forces someone to take the lead.

- How did it feel to try to solve the problems together?

- Did you feel more comfortable offering ideas and organising others, or being organised by others? Why might it be important to practise both of these roles?

- What was the biggest problem your group had? How did you deal with this?

Set-up

Grouping:
Groups of four or five.

Equipment needed:
None.

Space needed:
This game works best indoors as children may need to lie down on the floor. You only need a small space.

 Cross-curricular link

Ask the children to form numbers instead of letters. This provides the opportunity to ask mathematics questions, such as '9 minus 4' or '24 divided by 8'.

 **Set-up**

Grouping:
Groups of three or four.

Equipment needed:
Balls, bats, hoops, spots and a variety of larger equipment. Use what you have in the PE cupboard and aim for an interesting variety.

Space needed:
An interesting playground or any flat surface.

Crazy golf

Create your own hole and then play a round of golf.

How to facilitate the game

1 Show crazy golf. It'd be great to start this activity by showing a clip of crazy golf on the big screen in the classroom. That would be a good way of helping all children understand the concept of golf. If you can't do this, then quickly set up a simple hole with a spot to start on and a target to hit. Alternatively, you could use a drain in the playground or a chalk circle on the floor as a target. You can use noodles, rounders bats or tennis rackets as golf clubs.

2 Explain the game. Explain to the class that they are going to work as a group to create their own crazy golf hole. Show them the equipment available and remind them about your expectations of working together, including everyone and sharing equipment.

3 Play. Make groups of three or four children and begin. You could assign each group a certain amount of equipment. Give a time limit to design the hole, so the children have a chance to play later on. Once the holes are ready, groups can move around and try to play on each other's holes.

PE doesn't have to take place in a hall or playground. Consider how you might use other interesting spaces in your school.

Assessment for learning

In many cases, children may engage more with the process of creating their own hole than playing on another group's hole. This is an interesting reflection and it is worth exploring the difference between the creative and collaborative design process and the structured and competitive play experience.

● Which did you enjoy more: designing your own hole or playing on someone else's hole? Why?

● Which hole did you most enjoy playing on? What was particularly good about it?

Make it up

Pairs of children invent and create games using a variety of equipment.

How to facilitate the game

1 Get the equipment out! This activity provides an opportunity to get lots of equipment out of the PE cupboard. Get the children to help you. Get right into the back corners of the cupboard. Aim to get two or three of everything out, in particular a variety of bats, balls, spots, hoops and so on. If you are not sure what the equipment is or what it's used for, then definitely get it out! There should be enough for more than one piece of equipment per child. Arrange all the equipment in the centre of your PE area.

2 Explain the game. Explain to the class that they are going to invent and create their own games. They will move around the edge of the PE hall or playground, and when the teacher shouts, 'Go!', they will find a partner, go and get some equipment, and invent a game. (You may need to review expectations around finding a partner, working with others, sharing equipment, and playing safely.)

3 Play. Send children to the edge of the area. Ask them to move around in different ways (skipping, jogging backwards, hopping) and then shout, 'Go!' (You may need to help some children find partners. Perhaps you could have a designated zone where children with no partners can come and find one.)

4 Repeat. Give the children five minutes to create and play their game. Then ask them to put all the equipment back in the centre and repeat the activity. Next time, they can't choose the same partner and they can't use the same equipment.

Assessment for learning

This may take a while to set up, but it's amazing what the children can come up with. You want to aim to have about five or six repetitions of the activity before considering the questions below.

- What was more important to you: who you worked with, what you played, or how you played it?

- What makes a good game for you: a challenge, an opportunity to be with friends, or learning new skills?

- What kind of game do you enjoy so much that it doesn't matter who you play it with?

Aim

To consider what makes a positive play or movement experience.

Set-up

Grouping:
Whole class together.

Equipment needed:
Anything and everything!

Space needed:
Any.

Top TIP

This activity provides a useful assessment of how far your class has progressed this year. Keep a lookout for children who are good at creating new games, who are happy to work with others, who can share equipment and take turns, and who can apply movements in a variety of different games.

Aim

To reflect on the experience of physical activity when it happens outside of the traditional PE setting.

Set-up

Grouping:
Whole class together.

Equipment needed:
A tree, or somewhere designated as a base.

Space needed:
Get out of school and out of the usual places where PE takes place. Go to a park or wood – anywhere you can be in nature.

Forty forty

A whole-class tag game in the woods.

How to facilitate the game

1 Follow safety procedures and set boundaries. You will need to follow all the usual procedures and processes used when taking children off site. Make sure the class understand the area within which the game will take place.

2 Explain the game. Forty Forty is a traditional tag game. You will need to decide on a base, and this is typically a large tree, with a trunk that is safely accessible. The rules are:

- One child is chosen to be 'it'. (You could choose two or three children for a class of 30, or split the class and have three separate, smaller games happening.) All the other children run and hide while 'it' counts to 40.

- 'It' then needs to look for the other children, while the other children try to get back to the base tree without being spotted. If they make it back to base, they touch the tree and say, 'Forty forty, home' and they are safe.

- If 'it' spies another child, they say, 'Forty forty, I see <name>' and they need to race back to the base and touch the tree before the person whose name they have just called manages to get there. If they do this, then the child they spotted is out of the game.

3 Play. Decide who is 'it' and start the game. You may need to manage the children who make it successfully back to base or those who are caught. You could simply send them back out into the game to have another go. Alternatively, you could add a rule that anyone who makes it safely back to base can release two people who have been caught.

Assessment for learning

The idea of this game is to take PE out of the traditional hall or playground. This may need additional preparation work in terms of risk assessments if you are going off site, but the reward could be really engaging class play. Reflecting on this experience with the children may help them understand the link between PE and out-of-school movement experiences.

- How did it feel to do PE in a different setting to usual? What made it feel like this?

- What skills from this year's PE lessons did you use when playing the game?

Classroom debate

Which of these is the most powerful reason to want to move and play games: to compete, to be with friends or to learn something new?

Bingo

Complete the challenges to win the game.

How to facilitate the game

1 Introduce the game. Divide the class into teams of four or five children. In a class of 30, aim for six teams so you can have three games. Decide which games will be played. Not all games need to be the same, so you could have two teams playing football, another two playing rounders and another two playing volleyball. Give each team a whiteboard and pen.

2 Design the bingo card. Each team will use their whiteboard to design a bingo card of challenges for their opponents. They divide the whiteboard into nine squares using a three-by-three grid and write a challenge into each square. These challenges should be achievable and easy to understand. Importantly, they should be challenges that the opponents will enjoy completing. To create a set of holistic challenges, ask the class to include:

a. three sport challenges, e.g. hit a home run in baseball or do three passes in a row in netball
b. three social challenges, e.g. celebrate a goal together in football or play fairly and honestly for the whole game
c. three leadership challenges, e.g. invent a new rule that will make the game fairer or find a role for someone who isn't very involved in the game.

3 Play. Give each team their whiteboard of challenges and a pen. Play the game and have the whiteboards at the side of the pitches. Teams can tick off the challenges as they accomplish them. After ten minutes, give time for teams to discuss progress and think about how they will complete all the challenges.

Adaptations

For younger classes, make the bingo card in advance yourself, choosing simple tasks and challenges.

Assessment for learning

The challenges are useful because they allow children to be successful in a range of ways (not just by winning the game). The intention of this is to enhance inclusion and increase engagement.

The second question below may help some children consider the difference in experience and engagement when they are playing a game in order to achieve something specific that is not related to the score-line.

- Which kinds of challenges were hardest to come up with? Which kinds of challenges did you most want to accomplish?

- How was the experience of playing the game different from normal? Did you like this or not? Why?

Aim

To consider other people's needs and wants when designing game challenges.

Set-up

Grouping:
Teams of four or five.

Equipment needed:
This depends on the game, but you will probably want to use balls and bats. Each team will need a whiteboard and pen.

Space needed:
A netball court can host three games.

Aim

To try to learn a new game and reflect on this experience.

Set-up

Grouping:
Teams of five.

Equipment needed:
Each team will need one small ball and objects like tall cones or footballs to use as targets. Cones or spots can be used to mark out the areas.

Space needed:
A netball court could hold one to three courts, depending on the age of the children.

Tapu ae

A small-sided version of the traditional Maori handball game, suitable for Key Stage 2.

How to facilitate the game

1 Introduce this new game. Tell the children they are going to learn a new game. Tapu Ae (pronounced 'tapoo-why') is a traditional Maori handball game, played between two teams. There are some good videos online that explain the game and you could show these to the class as an introduction. The rules below reduce the team size down to five per team and simplify the game to make it easier for children to understand.

2 Explain the rules. The rules are as follows:

● The game is played with a ball called a Ki ('key'), a small ball that can easily be thrown and caught between the players. Each team has three Tupu – these are targets that the other team must hit with the Ki in order to score. For primary PE, you could make Tupu out of objects in the PE cupboard, such as tall cones, or balls balanced on cones.

● Each team should mark out a small circular area, called a Te Moto. This is where they will put their Tupu. One of their team members must stay in the Te Moto area to protect the Tupu. They are not allowed out of this area and no one else is allowed in.

● In between the two Te Moto areas, a long strip or zone called the Te Ao ('tey-ow') runs along the half-way line. This area divides the pitch into two halves and is a few metres wide. Each team should place one of their players in the Te Ao. Again, they are not allowed out of that zone and no one else is allowed in.

● That leaves three players on each team. One of these will remain in their own half, but won't be allowed in the Te Moto or Te Ao areas. The other two will be in the attacking half, but also prohibited from entering the Te Moto or Te Ao areas.

● The game is played quickly, by throwing the Ki between teammates, aiming to get the Ki to the two attackers so they can try to hit one of the Tupu. Importantly, the Ki must go through the player in Te Ao before a point can be scored. In the basic version of the game, players cannot run with the ball.

● If a player loses the ball or they throw it off the side of the pitch, possession is given to the other team. The game restarts after a point is scored (or after any dispute) by a referee throwing the ball from the side of the pitch into Te Ao.

3 Play. Have a go at the game. It may take a while for the children to understand it.

184

Assessment for learning

Don't focus on correcting techniques or tactics. Focus instead on reflecting on the experience of learning and playing a new game.

- What was it like to learn to play a new game? How did it compare with playing a game that you already know?

- What skills did you need in order to learn to play the game? Why might these skills be important in other areas of school and non-school life?

Tapu Ae

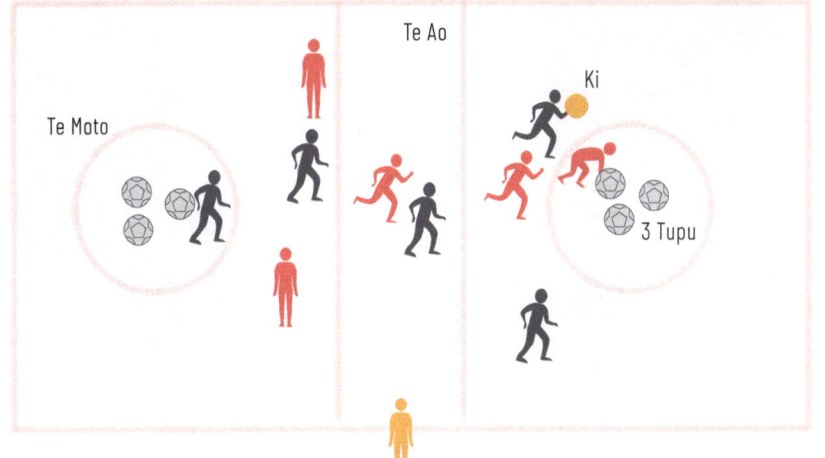

When you play games where children are locked into zones, there may be long periods when some children are completely uninvolved in the action. If this happens and you want to increase involvement levels, one option is to add another ball into the game and play with two balls instead of one.

June

Being part of a team

An introduction to being part of a team

Throughout our lives, we play important roles in many different teams. During this month, we help children recognise and consider the teams they are part of. This could of course be as part of a recognised sports team, but we also explore our responsibilities as part of a family group, a member of a class or school, and as part of a community or of wider society.

All the batters run at once in Diamond Strike (page 204).

'Teamwork' is often used in PE to describe a relay race activity or any game where children are grouped together. Rarely, however, are such activities accompanied by the assessment for learning necessary to explore and examine effective leadership and collaboration skills. In this month's games, we aim to develop the children's understanding of teamwork and their ability to be responsible, committed and supportive team members. In Noodle Rush (page 193), groups of children discuss 'success' and how this might be different from 'winning'; in Secret Agent (page 202), we consider the responsibility of leadership; and in Moving Target (page 198), we examine the kinds of positive behaviours that are necessary for teams to function well.

A note on team size: large-sided games tend to be dominated by the most confident players. It is difficult for many children to practise being part of a team when the main roles are shared among so many players. In ball games, the maximum team size should be five per team, but three-a-side might suit many children better. For younger classes, it is worth remembering that a pair of children working together is a team.

Key skills

- Helping teammates and seeking help from teammates
- Trusting each other
- Recognising our responsibility to our teammates
- Sacrificing yourself to help the team succeed
- Reminding each other of our commitment to the team
- Communicating positively
- Considering all the different teams we are part of, both in and out of school
- Leading effectively

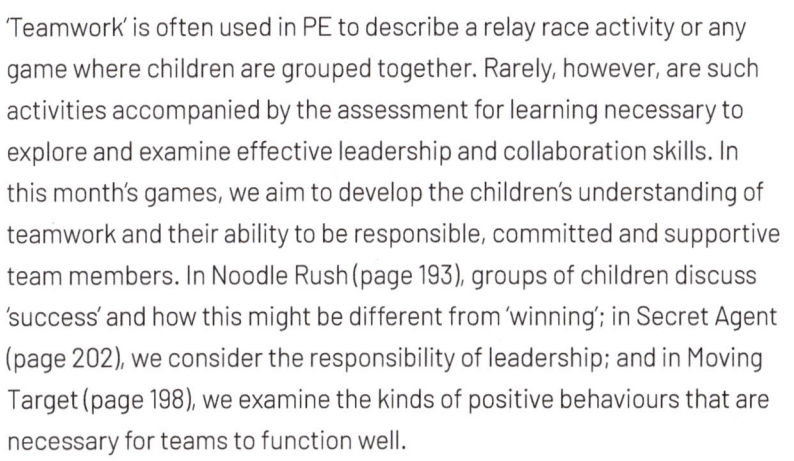

Four frameworks for facilitating dialogue between children

Dialogue between children is an essential part of the learning process. We need to take time in our PE lessons for children to reflect, consider and plan; to express their ideas; and to listen and share with others. Try using these four frameworks to support this.

1 Think, pair, share

Ask an engaging and challenging question. Give children time to consider the question, then tell children to discuss their answer with the person next to them. Walk around to overhear what they are saying and find out what ideas different children have. Pick on people to share their answers or ideas with the rest of the group.

2 Pose, pause, pounce, bounce

- **Pose.** Ask an engaging and challenging question. Ask the children to consider this question but say that you don't want any hands up.

- **Pause.** Wait until everyone has had time to consider the question and form a response.

- **Pounce.** Pick on someone to answer.

- **Bounce.** Whatever the response, without judging the response, 'bounce' it to someone else, for example, 'Zach, can you add to Amy's answer?'

3 Two stay, one goes

Ask an engaging and challenging question. Ask the children to discuss the answer in threes (or in their teams). The children then number themselves one to three in their groups. The number twos go to find a new group and tell this new group their original group's answers and ideas. The children then discuss these in their new group.

When in pairs, encourage children to sit opposite each other knee-to-knee to discuss and reflect.

4 Numbered heads together

When children are in small groups or teams, assign each child in each group with a different number, for example, one to five for a team of five children. Provide each number with a task relating to the game (this could be about solving a specific problem in the game or trying to achieve something in particular). After the children have explored the game for a while, group all the number ones together, all the number twos together and so on to allow them to discuss their own task more deeply.

Four ways for children to conduct self-assessment and peer assessment

Self-assessment and peer assessment are a crucial aspect of the learning process in PE. Here are four simple frameworks you can use to help children reflect on their own performance or progress – or on a classmate's.

1 Two stars and a wish

The children decide on two things that they (or their partner) are doing really well (two stars) and one thing that they could usefully improve (a wish). This method has the advantage of focusing on the positive aspects of performance.

2 Traffic lights

Choose a colour – red, amber or green – depending on how you feel you are doing (or how you feel your partner is doing). You could provide three coloured cones for children to select from. After they have chosen a colour, ask the children to explain why they chose it. This method allows children to consider their overall feeling first and then discuss in words why they feel that way.

3 Marks out of ten

Each team (or each individual within a team) gives themselves a mark out of ten depending on how they are doing (or how they feel another team is doing). You can then ask them, 'What would you need to do differently or better to get two marks higher? How will you achieve this?'

4 What's your superpower?

Using the language of video games, this approach asks the children to consider their superpower – the one thing they are doing really well (or one thing their partner is doing really well). It focuses on one positive thing they think they can do, which can then be shared among the group or team. You could also add in: 'What kind of cheat do you wish you could have for this game?' This question helps the children consider what they are finding most difficult.

Where space is limited, you may not be able to have everyone play games at once. Teams who are waiting for their turn can be given an observation task. Here, the green team is watching the red team and making notes on the way they communicate. Later they will give the red team feedback using two stars and a wish.

> ### Top TIP
> *Write the success criteria or the theme on a whiteboard. This helps to remind the children what to focus on in their self-assessment or peer assessment.*

Four roles for children who can't take part physically

Not all children can take part in PE every lesson. Some children might have an injury or condition that means they are unable to take part physically, for example. However, this needn't stop them from being part of the lesson or from accessing relevant learning. Here are four ways you can include children who can't take part physically.

1 Scorers and referees

Make sure the children can be heard and are listened to by those playing. It may be worth having a quick discussion about refereeing and how we treat referees and respect their decisions. This is a useful opportunity to help children understand and discuss their own feelings and reactions when a referee makes a poor decision.

2 Coaches

The children could help coach a team in a game or help coach the taggers in a tag game. Give the 'coach' a specific remit, otherwise what you usually get is just lots of shouting of instructions. For example, a 'coach' could usefully provide reminders to the team of their agreed strategy while they are playing, or link their role to the success criteria for the lesson.

3 Reporters

The children could observe a game and give a brief report on the action. Provide the reporter with two essential success criteria to report back on. For example, in Blindfold Boccia (page 192), they could report on how teammates support each other. They then have one minute to report back to the class.

4 Teaching assistants

Get them to help with setting out areas, handing out bibs, or putting children into teams. These children will then be involved in the learning, engaged in the lesson and actively developing their appreciation of the teaching process. You can extend this if you like with questions for them, such as: 'Which activity worked best today and why?' or 'What do you think the hardest part of being a teacher is?'

Triangle tag

Move and rotate to protect your teammate.

How to facilitate the game

1 **Demonstrate the game.** Ask three children to form a triangle by holding hands and facing each other. One of the children is the 'target'. A fourth child is the tagger and starts the game on the far side of the triangle, away from the target. The tagger starts the game by trying to move quickly round the triangle to tag the target player. The children in the triangle can rotate round to protect the target player from being tagged.

2 **Play.** The children will need to find a group of four, decide who the tagger and target are, and begin. Remind the children to change roles every so often, so everyone gets a chance to be the target and the tagger.

Adaptations

The target player could put a bib in their waistband. The tagger then needs to pull the bib to win the game. This can help avoid arguments relating to whether the tagger has successfully tagged the target player.

The children in the triangle could be joined with bibs rather than held hands. This works better for older classes where children may not want to hold hands with each other.

Assessment for learning

In this game, the three children in the triangle need to work together to protect the target child. They do this by rotating the triangle around so the target is as far as possible from the tagger.

● Children in the triangle need to communicate well with each other. How did you communicate with each other? (Answer: verbally, through eye contact or pulling arms.)

● What can you do with your triangle to make it harder for the tagger and to best protect your teammate? (Answer: make the triangle big by extending arms and moving backwards.)

 ### Aim

To move and communicate in a small team to protect a teammate.

Set-up

Grouping:
Groups of four.

Equipment needed:
None.

Space needed:
Any.

Top TIP

If you have limited space, or you notice that the triangles are running away from the tagger rather than rotating, you can put a spot or cone on the floor and ask the children forming the triangle to keep the spot within their triangle.

Aim

To explore the feelings of needing support and trusting others.

Set-up

Grouping:
Teams of three.

Equipment needed:
One chair and one target (e.g. a large skittle) per game, plus two or three throwing objects per player (e.g. beanbags, quoits, hoops or tennis balls).

Space needed:
Any.

Blindfold boccia

A challenging team version of the popular throwing or bowling game.

How to facilitate the game

1 Explain the game. The game is played between two teams. It is a version of bowls in which children attempt to throw or bowl an object so it lands closest to a target. In Boccia (pronounced 'botcha'), children throw from a seated position. Teams take it in turns to throw. The winning team is the one whose ball (or object) ends up closest to the target after all the balls have been thrown or bowled.

2 Demonstrate the game. The game begins with one of the players putting a target in the playing area. This could be a large skittle. The players and teams then take it in turns to sit on the chair and throw their objects, with the aim of landing the object as close as possible to the target.

3 Play. Children can form teams of three, find an opponent, and get the equipment they will need.

4 Reverse the chair. Once the children have had a go at the game, you can ramp up the challenge. Turn the chair around so it faces away from the target area. Throws must be overhead, behind the thrower, and made without looking. The thrower's teammates need to guide the thrower's aim using words only.

Assessment for learning

A team game of Boccia might be played by many children with little consideration to teammates or togetherness. However, by reversing the chair position, the game becomes a completely different experience. Success is now dependent on the team's ability to communicate with each other.

- How did your experience and feelings change when you couldn't see the target area?

- What support did you need from your teammates?

In this set-up, children are in groups of three and take it in turns to have three throws each. The thrower gets feedback from their teammates between each throw.

Noodle rush

Focus on speed in this small-team challenge.

How to facilitate the game

1 Show the game. Choose five children to demonstrate the game and ask them to stand in a small circle. Give each child a noodle and show them how to hold it so it stands upright in front of them. The challenge for the team is for them all to leave their noodle at the same time and race clockwise to get to the next person's noodle before it falls over (you will have to show them which way clockwise is). The team succeeds if they can all move clockwise successfully without any noodles falling down.

2 Play. Children can find their own teams, noodles and space.

Adaptations

To cater for different movement abilities, children can decide how far they stand from the next noodle. The gaps between noodles don't need to be even.

 You could try this with the whole class as one large team in one big circle. The circle could get bigger with a successful attempt and smaller with an unsuccessful attempt.

Assessment for learning

Many children might associate 'success' with 'winning'. However, in many games and activities, we can't win all the time. The questions below aim to help groups of children discuss what they want to achieve together in the game, and what they need to do well in order to achieve it.

- What is 'success' in this game? What do each of you need to do well in order to make this success happen?

- How might you work as a team to make sure everyone fulfils their responsibility?

- 'No one wins unless everyone wins.' What do you think this means? How does it relate to teamwork?

Aim

To define success and recognise your role and responsibility in this success.

Set-up

Grouping:
Groups of four or five.

Equipment needed:
One noodle per child.

Space needed:
Any.

Top TIP

To start a lesson or unit of work on being part of a team, ask the children to think of an example of a really good team. What does that team do well that makes them a team? Discuss in pairs and then as a class.

Spots on the floor might help children restart the activity themselves. They can also then move the spots to widen the circle as they become more successful.

Home alone

A steal-the-treasure game where teamwork is key.

How to facilitate the game

1 Demonstrate the game.
The game is based on the movie *Home Alone*, where Kevin is accidentally left at home by his family and needs to protect his house from burglars. Some tennis balls or beanbags (the treasure) are put in a hoop, which is guarded by one child in the group (Kevin). Kevin cannot stand inside the hoop. The other players (the thieves) need to work as a team to grab a piece of treasure without being caught. Kevin can tag a thief to catch them, and if this happens the tagged thief needs to retreat back five steps and can then re-join the game. This distance can be marked out using cones or spots.

2 Play. Children can choose their groups, get their equipment and decide who starts as Kevin.

Adaptations

↑ You want this game to be hard for the thieves, so they are forced to work together to succeed. If needed, you can make their task harder by adding a second Kevin so there are two children guarding the treasure.

Assessment for learning

This game has similar outcomes to Capture the Flag (page 161), where we explored how attacking movements can create spaces for teammates. The thieves need to work together to distract Kevin and open up spaces for others to grab the treasure. The questions and discussions below explore how winning is based on team effort. A player who sacrifices themselves to draw Kevin away from the hoop has played a vital role in the success of the team, even though they have been caught.

● How might you work together to get a chance to grab the treasure?

● 'If my teammate wins, I win.' What does this mean to you?

 Aim

To explore how everyone in a team contributes to success.

Set-up

Grouping:
Groups of four or five.

Equipment needed:
One hoop, four cones or spots, and five to ten tennis balls per group.

Space needed:
Any.

World domination

A whole-class tag game requiring communication and changes of loyalty.

Set-up

Grouping:
Whole class together.

Equipment needed:
None.

Space needed:
Any.

How to facilitate the game

1 Show the area. Show the boundaries of the playing area. Explain that the children are going to play a tag game within those boundaries and that they are not allowed out of that area.

2 Explain the rules. Each child should think of a country. Ask them to try to think of a country no one else will think of. During the tag game, each child needs to tag others on their back and not allow their backs to be tagged by others. If they tag someone else on their back, then they tell them their country and the tagged person now becomes that country too.

3 Play. Ask them to spread around the area, and then shout, '3-2-1, play!' to begin. You could play for a limited time (the winning team being the country with most people at the end), or until only one country remains.

You may need to remind some children of the rules, as some may forget in the excitement of the game. Play once before reflecting and then have another game.

Assessment for learning

When a child tags someone else on the back, the tagged child joins their team. They need to leave behind the loyalties they had to whatever team they were previously representing and try to succeed as part of their new team. Some children might find this transition from one team to another difficult. Other children might allow themselves to be tagged so they can join their friends' team. It is worth reflecting on this with the following questions.

● How did you feel when you were tagged and had to switch to a new team?

● Why is loyalty important when you are part of a team? When is loyalty not such a good thing?

Cross-curricular link

There are obvious links to geography in the game as described here. But the game doesn't have to be played with countries. It could work just as well by asking all the children to choose historical figures or characters from a book the class is reading.

Rob the nest

An easily adaptable team game with a focus on working together.

How to facilitate the game

1 **Show the area.** Each team will have a nest, which is their home area. A nest could be a hoop, or a small square marked out by cones. Set up the nests so they are in a circle formation all roughly equidistant from the next. In the middle of the area, or scattered around, are lots of different types of ball.

2 **Explain the game.** Each team needs to try to fill their nest with balls. The team that collects the most balls wins. To get a ball, simply run over to it, pick it up and bring it back to your nest. Importantly, all team members can go at the same time – no waiting your turn!

3 **Play.** Once all teams are ready at their empty nests, say, 'Go!'

4 **Progress.** Once all the balls have gone from the middle area, teams can start stealing from each other's nests. Children are not allowed to guard the nest nor tackle each other.

Adaptations

↑ Test the children's ability to work together by restricting them to moving each ball using netball rules (where you can't travel with the ball). Children will need to move to support each other in order to get a ball back to their nest.

↑ For older classes of children, add an option for one of each team to guard the treasure and tag invaders, or for tackling to be allowed in certain areas (if playing with feet or bouncing).

Assessment for learning

Play the game without any additional rules to begin with. Then give the children a chance to explore how they work together, using the questions below. Finally, ask each team to come up with a key word that sums up their commitment to each other in the game.

● What responsibility do you have to your teammates in this game?

● How might you remind each other of this responsibility during play?

Aim

To consider the commitment we make to our teammates in team games.

Set-up

Grouping:
Teams of four or five.

Equipment needed:
Cones, markers or a hoop to denote each team's nest. Lots of assorted balls, at least one per child.

Space needed:
Any.

Rob the Nest

Top **TIP**

This activity is ideal for using the 'one person who...' structure (see page 79). For example: one person who can only use their feet to move the ball; one person who must bounce the ball; and one person who must encourage others while playing.

Moving target

A popular target practice activity, used in schools 100 years ago.

Aim

To explore the positive behaviours of an effective team.

Set-up

Grouping:
Split the class into four equal-sized teams.

Equipment needed:
One large ball as a target (the larger the better!); plus at least one soft tennis ball per child.

Space needed:
The area size will depend on the throwing capacity of the children.

How to facilitate the game

1 Show the area. This game takes place on a large square court, with one team working along each side of the square. A football (or large ball) is placed in the middle of the square and tennis balls are divided up amongst the teams. Each team attempts to drive the football towards one of their opponents' lines by hitting it with tennis balls. As soon as the football crosses over a team's line, a point is awarded to each of the opposing teams, and the game can restart.

2 Explain the game. Split the class into four equal-sized teams and send each team to a side of the square. Children must throw from the line on their side of the square. If a ball lands inside the square, it may be retrieved by the closest team as long as the game is not interfered with.

3 Play. Once the rules are clear and everyone is ready, start the game with a '3-2-1, play!'.

Adaptations

You could reduce this game down to a two-a-side game played on a very small court. Alternatively, you could play several games next to each other (as in the photo). It really depends on your space and what you think will work best for your class.

Assessment for learning

Some children may have a more accurate or powerful throw than others, but success in this game will be achieved through many small victories. That is what makes this game interesting and engaging: everyone has a role to play.

The questions below get children thinking about being a good teammate. It may also be worth considering what teams the children currently consider themselves a part of. In school, this could be their reading group or their music group. Out of school, it could be their family.

- What examples were there of positive communication in the game? How might this kind of communication help?

- Who was a good teammate in the game? What did they do that was good?

- Can you think of a team that you are part of where you need the support of others in order to succeed?

Cross-curricular link

This game appeared in the UK government's 1933 PE manual for teachers. What do the children think PE lessons would have been like at school nearly 100 years ago?

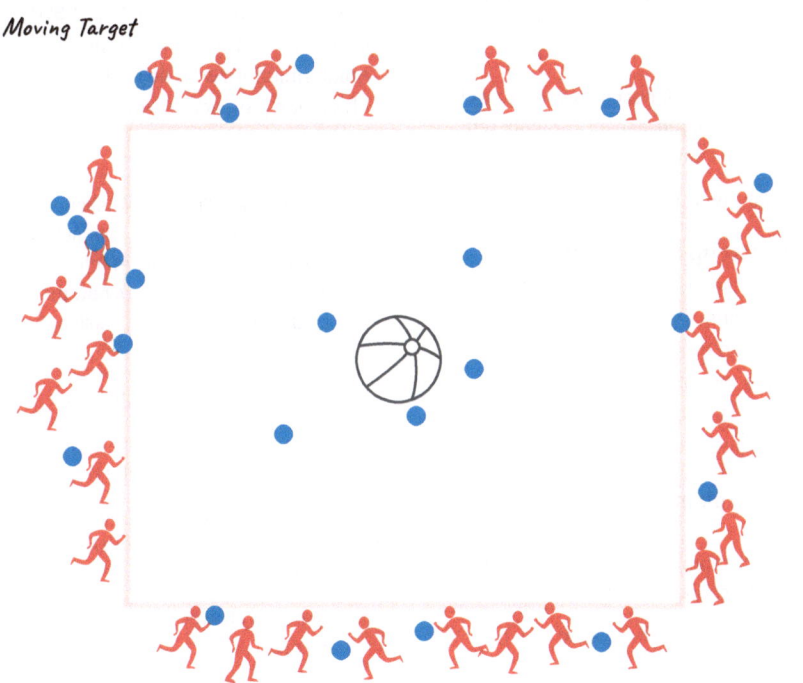

Moving Target

An alternative set-up: three games side-by-side with a team at each end of each court.

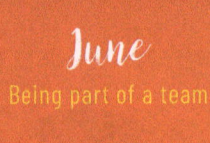

Aim

To consider what a team is and what makes an effective team.

Set-up

Grouping:
Teams of three or four.

Equipment needed:
12 different-coloured crayons hanging at assorted locations in your playground; 12 different maps, each showing the location of one of the crayons (print two copies of each map); one scorecard per team; optional: challenge cards and assorted equipment.

Space needed:
A large, interesting playground area or outdoor space.

Playground orienteering

Decision-making and challenge are added to this traditional favourite.

How to facilitate the game

1 Prepare in advance. This activity takes quite a lot of preparation before the lesson.

- Start by drawing a map of your playground area.

- Make a copy of the map and use a number to indicate the location of a hidden crayon.

- Hide the crayon at that location in the playground, tied to a piece of string. So, for example, the purple crayon is number six and this is hidden under the slide. There is a number six on the map, exactly where the slide is.

- Repeat this for each crayon. For a class of 30 children, aim for 12 numbered crayons and associated maps.

- Make two copies of each map.

2 Set up a base area. Have a base area, where you will keep all the maps. Teams will take and return maps to this area. This is also a good place for you to position yourself, to keep track of progress and to help teams that need it.

3 Explain the game.

- Each team of three or four children get a scorecard.

- They take one numbered map from the box.

- They must use the map to locate the crayon and use the crayon to colour in the appropriately numbered box on their scorecard.

- Then they can return the map to the box and take a map for another crayon.

- The winning team will be the first to complete the scorecard correctly.

4 Play. Have a go at this simple version of the game. Tell teams they need to come and check in with you after they have completed two numbered maps. This allows you to check they have understood the rules or to provide quick finishers with an extra challenge (see adaptations).

Adaptations

Have a lucky-dip box of challenge cards. Once a team has completed two numbers, they take a new challenge card each time they collect a new map. The cards will have specific challenges, for example:

- You can't take the map with you.

- You must take a ball to the crayon and use netball rules for moving it.

- One of your team is blindfolded and must be instructed to get to the crayon – you can't touch them.

- You are not allowed to speak to each other.

Assessment for learning

It is worth reflecting on what we mean by the word 'team'. Try to get children thinking about the teams they are part of and what roles they play in these teams.

- How would you define a team? What teams are you part of in school or out of school? Is your class a team? Is your school a team? Is your family a team?

- What makes an effective team? How do you know if you are part of a team that is effective? Were you an effective team during this game?

Classroom debate

How do you help classmates become teammates?

or

What's the most important team you are part of?

Ask children to come and check with you after they have completed two numbered maps. You can then provide feedback and increase the challenge level if needed.

201

Aim

To consider what effective leadership looks like in team challenges.

Set-up

Grouping:
Teams of four or five.

Equipment needed:
14 cones or markers to make seven 'gates' on the floor. Optional: two whiteboards per game and assorted balls (one per child).

Space needed:
This game can work in a small hall, although it will be better in a larger area.

Secret agent

Deceit and espionage meet quick movements and teamwork in this spy-based team tag game.

How to facilitate the game

1 **Show the area.** This activity takes place on a court with a small safe zone at each end. Between the two safe zones are three rows of gates. Each gate is made up of two markers of the same colour, about two metres apart. The rows nearest the safe zones have two gates each, and the middle row has three gates.

2 **Add the children.** Once set up, ask the children to practise travelling from one safe zone to the other, moving in creative ways through the three rows of gates. You could have all the children move at the same time (i.e. they leave the safe zone when they like). Alternatively, you could send the children off from the safe zone in quick succession in batches of five.

Challenge them: 'Who can show me the most creative and interesting ways of moving?'

3 **Add guards.** We will now add security guards to protect the gates. Have one guard for the rows nearest the safe zones – they will need to guard both gates on these rows. Have two guards protecting the three gates in the middle row. The guards must move to block the gates and can tag people as they try to get through. If you are tagged, you need to go back and try again.

4 **Make teams of four.** Ask the children travelling through the gates to get into teams of four and secretly identify one of their team to be the secret agent. The team's job is to get their secret agent from one safe zone to another as often as possible. They get a point every

Secret Agent

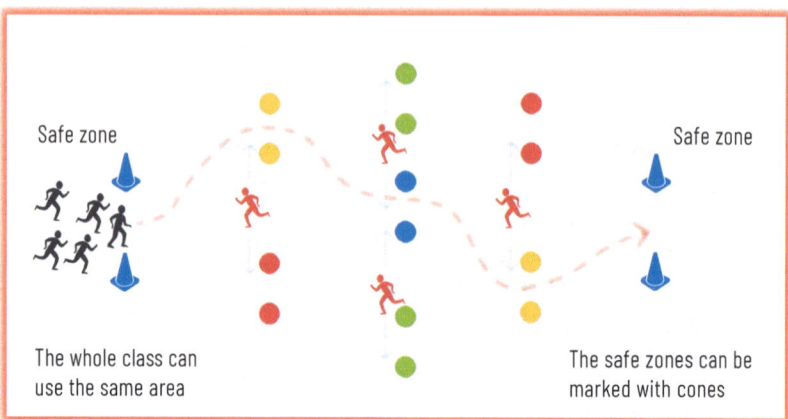

Safe zone

Safe zone

The whole class can use the same area

The safe zones can be marked with cones

time they can do this. They can change secret agents when they get to a safe zone. You could have a whiteboard at each safe zone to record scores.

Adaptations

↑ You could add a ball for the children to travel with and allow the children to choose how they travel with it.

Assessment for learning

This game is complicated to explain all at once. Follow the steps shown, adding and progressing only once the children have understood each stage. Once the game has progressed to include the secret agent, you can start to discuss the teamwork elements involved. The second question starts exploring what effective leadership looks like within a team.

● What must you do well to get your secret agent across safely?

● Who made most decisions in your team? Who took on the role of leader in your team? Why was it that person? What was good about their leadership?

✚ **Set-up**

Grouping:
Teams of four or five.

Equipment needed:
Chalk, cones or markers to mark out the court, plus one tennis ball per game to play with.

Space needed:
Multiple small courts. A class of 30 will need three or four courts. (See the diagram on page xvii.)

Diamond strike

A small-sided baseball game for Key Stage 2.

How to facilitate the game

1 Set up the courts. Each court will need a diamond marked out by chalk or by using cones or markers. One point of the diamond will be the striking area where the ball is hit from. If you're using multiple courts for one class, have all the striking areas together in the centre of the area, each facing in different directions into the corners of the area (see diagram on page xvii).

2 Show the game. Each diamond hosts one game, played between two teams of four to five players. One team is the fielding team and one is the batting team. Players on the batting team take it in turns to hit the ball into the diamond area. They do this by throwing the ball with one hand and striking or slapping the ball with the other hand. The batting team then attempts to run around the diamond while the fielding team retrieves the ball.

3 Everyone runs! Unlike normal rounders or cricket, in this game, everyone on the batting team runs together! So, once the batter has struck the ball into the area, all members of the batting team who are waiting for their turn to bat leave the batting area, aiming to run around the diamond. They must run together, so they are only as fast as their slowest player.

4 How to score. The batting team can stop safely at any of the points of the diamond on the way round. But if they are running towards a point and the fielding team returns the ball to that point before the batting team gets there, then the batting team must return to the batting area having scored no points. If the batting team stays at one of the points, they are safe. In this instance, the next person to bat should leave the group and return to the batting area for their turn to bat (they will run alone after they've hit the ball). Those who are left can move again when the ball is next struck by one of the batting team. If they can make it all the way round the diamond, they each get a point for their team.

5 Play. Play so that each of the batting team has two turns to bat, before swapping the batting and fielding teams round.

Using tees helps all children to succeed in striking the ball. You could give children a bat to strike the ball instead of asking them to use their hands.

Assessment for learning

Points are scored in this game by making it around the diamond. It doesn't matter whether players do this in one hit or move from one point to the next over two or three hits. So, it should get to a stage where players are waiting on points of the diamond when the batter hits the ball. You could draw this situation on a whiteboard and discuss options with the following questions.

● When you are the batter, where could you hit the ball so it helps your teammates get round the diamond safely?

● Why is it important to think of your teammates when playing a team game? Can you think of any other examples when you have been part of a team that needs to think of others in order to be successful?

Top TIP

When you do striking and fielding games, have a bucket of different-sized bats and balls available so children can choose an option that they are comfortable with.

Competing as a team

An introduction to competing as a team

In the two short pages that make up the PE National Curriculum for KS1 and KS2, competing or competition is mentioned six times. Competing with others can be really enjoyable and can provide contexts to practise, develop and use skills. Reflecting on competition experiences – when the chance is taken to do so – offers the teacher a chance to discuss feelings, values and desires and to help children to grow and thrive.

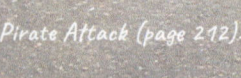

Pirate Attack (page 212).

However, we need to be careful about how we serve competitive experiences, as they often only nourish the few who are already good at competing. Many children find their PE diet tasteless and bland if competition is unaccompanied by the added delicacies of kindness, empathy and respect. Any potential benefits of competition are unfulfilled if the children are put off altogether by the atmosphere and environment in which the competition takes place.

What meaning and power does competition have for the likely future lives of the children? The world is a competitive place and we need to equip children to be able to deal with this. We should also work with children to explore how competition could be more ethical, fair and equitable.

Building on the work of previous chapters, games this month focus on team competition. Some of this month's quick starters can easily be progressed to take up a whole lesson. For example, team tactics are explored in Magic Three (page 214) and setting targets in Three-Team Bulldog (page 213).

On page 222, we explore the Sport Education approach and how this could be used over a unit of work or to link PE and extra-curricular sport and develop competitions.

Key skills

- Recording team scores and setting targets (evaluating and recognising success)
- Comparing performances with previous ones and demonstrating improvement
- Keeping self and others motivated
- Being determined and overcoming setbacks
- Understanding responsibility and loyalty when competing in a team
- Competing respectfully
- Exploring equality, equity and ethics in team competition
- Experiencing and reflecting on a variety of playing and non-playing roles in competitive sport

Four ways to record the score in games

Keeping score may help children to understand how they are doing in relation to another team, to explore winning and losing, and to identify teams that are struggling and teams that need an extra challenge. Here are four ways in which the children can record their team's score.

1 Children record their own score on a whiteboard

This might work best if only the point-scorer can go to the board to add the score and the game continues while they are gone (i.e. don't wait for them to return before restarting). If there are many score-related arguments during the game, give each team a separate whiteboard.

2 Practise numeracy skills

Link PE scoring to the mathematics the children are doing in class. So, if they are working on multiplying by three and five in the classroom, make each goal worth three points, and later add in a special way of also scoring five points. As well as practising their numeracy skills, the children are more likely to remember what score they are on.

3 Use levels

In video games, progress is often indicated by what level you are playing at. Beginner players will start at Level 1, where key fundamental moves and concepts can be explored. Later, as children increase in ability and confidence, they can move up the levels. Critically, in many video games, children may choose the level they are playing at. So, rather than keeping score, perhaps experiment with having levels instead. For example, in a modified handball game, Level 2 might be achieved after scoring two goals. On Level 2, players must only use one hand to throw and catch.

4 Beanbags in hoops

It is sometimes a good variation to keep score using physical objects. Beanbags are good for this because they don't roll or blow away in the wind. Each team can have a hula hoop near their goal, and each time someone scores a point or goal, they bring a beanbag and put it into their hoop. If you don't have many beanbags, each team can start with two beanbags and steal one from the other team's hoop when they score a point.

Mini whiteboards can be really useful in PE. Groups can record their score, plan tactics and evaluate their progress.

Grouping by ability

There are many arguments for and against ability grouping in the classroom. Many of these arguments are also relevant in PE. However, the additional physical element of PE makes things a bit different. Here, we will examine the two sides of the debate and then consider some tips for ability grouping if you do decide to go down this route.

The case for ability grouping in PE

Games in PE can be physically competitive and these kinds of game might serve some children better than others. In ball games, for example, someone is often trying to steal the ball from you or to stop the ball from reaching you. This means that access to the enjoyment and learning in games can be dependent on physical and technical abilities (those who are quickest and strongest might get much more opportunity to do things with the ball). In many PE lessons, children with lower physical and technical ability and confidence are least involved while those with more advanced skills dominate (yet are often unchallenged).

The case against ability grouping in PE

As adults, most of our movement opportunities take place with a wide range of other people. The 'real world' is mixed ability and children need to get used to managing themselves and their games within that context. If the teacher has been able to teach the children the skills of inclusion, the less able can learn from the most able. This can happen if the children adapt games to include everyone and manage differences by adjusting rules or roles. Labelling children as low ability can be damaging to their confidence and how they perceive themselves. We need to make sure that how we group children doesn't result in some children seeing themselves as less worthy or as having less potential.

Top tips if you decide to try ability grouping

- First, consider: *what ability?* If you're doing a piece of work on problem-solving, and using modified netball as the vehicle to explore that, then which set of abilities is our grouping based on: the ability to solve problems or the technical ability to play netball? The 'best' netball player might not be the one with the most advanced problem-solving skills.

- Don't label the children 'high ability' or 'low ability'. If you do use ability groupings, don't make them obvious. Instead, a strategic teacher could let the children choose their groups or teams and then sneakily switch a few children around while the game is in action in order to respond to individual children's needs for higher or lower challenge.

- Don't group in the same way all the time. Mix it up. Children should have the experience of playing and learning alongside a range of different children.

- Whatever groupings you use, there will be differences between children within the group. Plan in advance for how you'll add challenge and support for individuals.

July

Competing as a team

QUICK STARTER GAME 1

Aim

To explore and compare effort levels when competing with others.

Set-up

Grouping:
Groups of four or five.

Equipment needed:
One noodle and two mats per group.

Space needed:
An indoor surface.

Pull your weight

A two-against-two pulling battle.

How to facilitate the game

1 Arrange the mats. Ask your class to help you set up pairs of mats next to each other, so their shorter sides are touching. For a class of 30 you will need six pairs of mats.

2 Show the game. Demonstrate with one group using one pair of mats. Ask for four children to demonstrate, two on each mat. Tell each pair to hold different ends of the same noodle. On the count of three, the pairs will pull the noodle, and try to pull the other pair onto their mat to win the game. (If your pair both let go of the noodle, you lose.)

3 Play. Children should make groups of four or five. If they have a group of five, they can take turns to referee. Make sure the children play safely.

4 Add challenge. Once the children have had a few turns at the game, challenge them to choose who the strongest player is and see what happens when the strongest player plays on their own against two or three others. Can the group find a way of splitting the players so there is an equal force at either end of the noodle?

Assessment for learning

In team sport psychology, the Ringelmann effect suggests that individual levels of effort decrease as team size increases. So, in this game, could it be that children make more effort to pull the noodle when they are on their own compared with when they are in a team of two or three? The following questions reflect on the children's experience and explore the commitment we need to make when we are part of a team.

- What was the difference between pulling the noodle on your own compared with pulling the noodle as a pair or three? When did you make the most effort and try the hardest?

- Under what circumstances might you make more or less effort when you are part of a team?

More information

- Ingham, A. G., Levinger, G., Graves, J. and Peckham, V. (1974), 'The Ringelmann effect: Studies of group size and group performance', *Journal of Experimental Social Psychology*, 10, (4), 371–384.

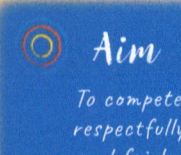

Aim

To compete respectfully and fairly.

Set-up

Grouping:
Teams of four or five.

Equipment needed:
One noodle per child.

Space needed:
Any.

Pirate attack

The children sword fight as a team in this swashbuckling pirate adventure.

How to facilitate the game

1 Demonstrate the game. Ask for a volunteer and give them a noodle to hold like a sword. Hold a noodle yourself too. Demonstrate a pirate sword fight. You get a point if you are able to touch your noodle against your opponent on the knee or below. Make it clear that you are not allowed to aim for the upper body or head.

2 Play. You could begin this game by playing one against one, so children get used to the concept. Alternatively, you could go straight into the team version below.

3 Demonstrate the team version.

- Each team of four or five pirates will choose a captain and give them a pirate-sounding name, like Saida the Sea Blazer or Max the Mighty.

- The captain will not have a noodle. The aim is to tag the opposing team's captain in order to win the game. The pirates can do this by hitting the captain with the noodle on or below the knee. The other pirates can protect their captain.

- If a pirate is hit below the knee, they need to stand balanced on the other leg until unfrozen by a tag of a teammate.

- The game could take place in an assigned square on the floor, as this allows the teams to position their captain in the corner. You could play one team against another, or all teams against each other.

4 Play. Give children time to consider some tactics and name their captain. Once a captain has been tagged, the team can start playing again straight away with a different captain. To keep score, each team starts with five points and loses a point each time their captain is tagged.

Assessment for learning

This is a good opportunity to revisit some of the concepts we first looked at back in September: following rules and playing fairly and honestly.

- How might it feel if you tag someone on or below the knee and they ignore this and carry on playing?

- Why is it important to respect the rules when we compete together?

- What might you do if you think someone has broken the rules? (See page 21.)

> ## Top TIP
> When you buy noodles, they are usually very long. It helps to cut them in half for this kind of game (and for most PE games).

Three-team bulldog

Work together to set a target as a team in this dodging and racing game.

How to facilitate the game

1 Show the area. Show the perimeter of a large rectangle that the game will be played in. A netball court would work well. Split the class into three teams. Send one team to each end of the area and arrange one tagging team in the middle of the area. Give each team a name or a number.

2 Demonstrate the game. Call the name of one of the teams at the end of the area. This team must run and dodge to the other end of the area without getting tagged on the way. The running team gets a point for every person who arrives at the other end without getting tagged. Once the first running team has had their turn, ask the taggers to reset themselves, and call the name of the other team. (After that turn, you can change the tagging team in the middle and replay in the same way.)

3 Change the scoring system. This game has a complex scoring system, designed to challenge teams to set targets together:

- Before each turn, the running team needs to declare how many children they predict will get to the other side successfully without being tagged.

- If they manage to achieve this or better this, they can treble that prediction as their score. (Note: they don't treble the number of children who got across

successfully, rather they treble their predicted number.)

- If they don't manage to achieve their prediction, they get one point per child who gets across safely.

Adaptations

↑ If you want to increase the complexity further, you could have both the running teams run at once.

↑ You could also add a bib tail to each of the taggers, so runners can add to their score by stealing bibs along the way.

Assessment for learning

The teaching and learning in this game should focus on the scoring system. Children may work out that they are better off predicting a small number and achieving it, rather than predicting a large number and failing to reach it. The first question might be asked mid-activity, once the children have got used to the rules. It should prompt discussion about how the children help each other get across the area. The second question could be used after the activity to reflect on the importance of setting targets.

- What do you need to do better or differently in order to increase the number of players who get across successfully?

- Why is setting targets important when you are trying to improve? Ask the children to think of examples from non-PE subjects.

Aim
To set team targets to achieve and improve on.

Set-up

Grouping:
Three teams of approximately equal numbers.

Equipment needed:
None.

Space needed:
Any.

Aim

To work as a team to evaluate the success of different tactics.

Set-up

Grouping:
Teams of three.

Equipment needed:
Assorted different-coloured beanbags or knotted bibs (one per child); plus nine hula hoops per game. Optional: cones or markers.

Space needed:
Any.

Magic three

Quick thinking is needed in this tactical small-team throwing game.

How to facilitate the game

1 Show the area. Set up nine hula hoops in a three-by-three grid. Have a team of three children along each side of the grid (so four teams in total). Each child has a beanbag. This works well if each team's beanbags are a different colour. (You could tie bibs in a knot if you don't have enough beanbags.) If you have additional children, assign them as referees and score-keepers, and rotate these children into the game after a few turns.

2 Demonstrate the game. The game begins with the referee shouting, 'Play!' Every child must throw their beanbag, aiming for their team to make a line of three connected hoops. They are not allowed to use the hoops nearest to them unless they make a diagonal line. If a team successfully lands their beanbags inside three different hoops to make a line of three, they get a point.

3 Play. For older classes, you may need to increase the distance they throw from (if it's too easy). You can put a cone or two for children to stand behind, for example.

Adaptations

↑ For older classes, introduce an extra challenge for extra points: you get ten points if you make a line of three and your beanbags are the only ones in those hoops. This includes a line of three that is made and exists just temporarily before other teams throw their beanbags.

Magic Three

Assessment for learning

In order to succeed, children will need to work with their teammates to discuss and decide which line of three to aim for and which person will be responsible for getting each hoop. These questions focus on this communication.

- How did you know which hoop to aim for?

- Was it easier to go for a straight line or a diagonal line?

If the game has been progressed with the extra 'ten-point' challenge, it becomes a lot more tactical. For example, it might be better to throw early and get a quick line of three for ten points. Or it might be wise to throw just one beanbag to disturb other teams' lines and delay your other throws until the end when you can see which hoops are empty. This predicament allows us to explore tactical decision-making as a team.

- What are the risks and benefits of throwing early, as soon as the referee says, 'Play'?

- How many different tactics did you try? How do you know which one worked best for you?

Top TIP

In order to make activities more child-centred, ask the children to come up with their own scoring systems or progressions. After you have shown the basic game of Magic Three, the children may have some great ideas for how it could be developed.

July
Competing as a team

QUICK STARTER GAME 5

Aim

To consider the effect of the score-line on motivation in team competition.

Set-up

Grouping:
Teams of three.

Equipment needed:
Each game will need one dice, one ball and a small area with a line at each end (this can be either a line on the floor or marked out with cones or spots).

Space needed:
Each game can be played on a small court.

3v3 line ball

Explore how the score-line affects your feelings and motivation.

How to facilitate the game

1 Demonstrate the game. The initial set-up for this game is simple: a team of three plays another team of three in any invasion game they choose. There is a line at each end of the court, which each team is trying to get to. Instead of goals or baskets to score in, teams get a point if they can stop the ball on the end line.

2 Explain the scoring. Each team starts by rolling a dice. That is their starting score. Whenever they score a point, they have a choice of either adding one to their score, or replacing their score with a roll of the dice.

3 Play. Play the game for five minutes, then switch teams and restart.

Assessment for learning

When playing competitive games, the motivation and mood of children (and adults!) are often heavily influenced by the score-line. A team that is losing by many points may become disheartened and stop trying.

The scoring system in this game exposes children to a variety of different score-lines. The game therefore provides the opportunity to consider the effect of the score-line on team performance in competition.

● How did it feel to be winning compared to losing? How would you describe the feeling when you overtake your opponents' score?

● Does the score-line affect the way we play as a team?

● How might we control our emotions and motivation so we consistently play our best regardless of the score?

 Cross-curricular link

For older children, you could use the scoring system in this game to explore probability by asking:

● If you have a score of one, would you add another point or replace it with the dice score?

● What if you have a score of six? What about a score of three?

Bullseye

A competitive team game involving blocking and intercepting.

How to facilitate the game

1 Show the area. The game takes place in and around a circle on the floor marked out by spots or cones. Inside this large circle is a smaller circle. The exact sizes of circles will depend on the throwing and catching ability of the children. You will probably need three areas like this set up for a class of 30 children.

2 Demonstrate the game. The game is played in teams of three. One team of three will play against two other teams of three, then switch round.

- One team of three children will be the blocking team. They are only allowed in the area between the two circles.

- Two other teams will join up to make a team of six throwers. Five of them will spread out around the outside edge of the large circle, with a sixth player inside the smaller circle in the middle.

- None of the throwing players are allowed into the blockers' area.

- The throwers have a tennis ball and they need to throw and catch the tennis ball, trying to throw it into the middle player. The ball can only be thrown under shoulder height.

- The blockers' job is to block the pass into the middle player and try to intercept any passes going in and out of the middle circle.

3 Play. Once the children have had a go at the game and understood the rules, introduce a scoring system. The throwing team gets a point each time they get the ball in and out to the middle player successfully. The blocking team gets a point each time they intercept a pass successfully. The teams take turns being a team of three blockers. Which blocking team can be most successful?

Adaptations

For younger classes, try using a bib tied in a knot rather than a ball. It is easier to catch and they may be more successful.

Assessment for learning

We might use this game to explore the experience of being in unfair competition. The team of three blockers is playing against a team of six. They are outnumbered and may find this task difficult. If you really want to extend their challenge, try introducing a second ball to the game.

- How did it feel to be a team of three playing against a team of six?

- What kind of attitude do you need in order to cope well in this situation?

- When might you find yourself being outnumbered in real sport? (Possible answer: in invasion games if someone gets sent off.)

Aim

To explore feelings of competing when we are outnumbered in a difficult task.

Set-up

Grouping:
Teams of three.

Equipment needed:
Each game will need spots or cones to mark out a circle on the floor, plus one ball.

Space needed:
Any.

Bullseye

High v low basketball

A simple, but deliberately unfair, game of basketball.

Set-up

Grouping:
Teams of three or four.

Equipment needed:
Two hula hoops and one large bouncy ball per game; bibs or string to tie each hula hoop to a fence.

Space needed:
Four or five small courts, each with a fence (or similar) at both ends where the hula hoops can be tied.

How to facilitate the game

1 Show the court. This basketball game takes place on a small court, with a hoop at each end. Show the children the boundaries of the court.

2 Explain the game. The game is a simplified version of basketball. The only rules to follow are that the ball must be bounced in order to move with it. This is called dribbling. The ball can also be passed to a teammate.

3 Scoring. The hoops should be tied to a fence (or other structure or object) to form a goal at each end of the court. You can tie the hoops with bibs or string. A team can score a point by shooting the ball into the hoop at their end of the court. In this game, we are going to explore fairness, equality and equity. In order to do this, we are going to make the game deliberately unfair. For one team, tie the hula hoop high up on the fence, so it is hard to score into. For the other team, tie the hula hoop low down on the fence, so it is easy to score into.

Adaptations

↑ For older children, you could limit them to one dribble per possession – so they can't stop dribbling and then restart again.

↑ You could limit each child to five bounces per dribble in order to encourage passing.

Assessment for learning

Although the rules of this game are the same for each team (and therefore equal), the experience of success is different for each team due to the different height of their hoop. Teach the children that the rules of play may be equal but the game is not equitable. (If you really want to exaggerate this, you could mix the teams up so all the tall players are on one team shooting in the low hoop, and shorter players are together aiming for the high hoop.)

The questions below can be adjusted or added to depending on the age and stage of the children.

● Was the game fair? Why or why not? How might you adjust the game to make it fairer?

● Are there things you can think of in school that are unfair or unequal?

● What kinds of barriers or differences are there in society that prevent some people from having equal or equitable access? What can we do to make things fairer?

TopTIP

If you don't have a fence to tie a hoop onto, here are some alternatives:

- *You could use a spot on a wall or draw a circle with a piece of chalk on a wall.*

- *You could use a 'target' player instead. This is one of the team who needs to stand at the end of the court holding a hoop that the ball needs to be thrown through.*

Classroom debate

'A competitive world is better than a collaborative world.'

Do you agree or disagree?

Aim
To explore different roles in competitive sport.

Set-up

Grouping:
Teams of four or five.

Equipment needed:
Four benches, two small balls and bibs for teams.

Space needed:
Two small pitches.

Benchball

An exciting team competition, perfect for indoor PE halls.

How to facilitate the game

1 Show the area. Each pitch needs one bench at both ends. A player from each team stands on one of the benches.

2 Demonstrate the game.

- The game is a throwing and catching game, like netball, and points are scored when a team successfully throws the ball to their player on the bench.

- When this happens the player who threw the ball takes the place of the player on the bench, and the game is resumed by them throwing the ball to someone on the opposite team.

- The games will take place between two teams of four or five players each.

3 Set up. Two games will take place at once, each game lasting ten minutes. Four teams will play at any time. Children in the fifth team will divide the following roles between them:

- referee
- score-keeper
- scout (they should observe the teams playing and identify key strengths and areas for improvement).

Assessment for learning

The following questions are intended to reflect on the children's experience once they have had the opportunity to explore the approach.

- Did you prefer playing the game or one of the other roles? Why?

- Why are non-playing roles important for sport to take place?

An upper KS2 class play Benchball in a very small space.

Cross-curricular link

Classroom work could involve match reports being written and numeracy work producing league tables.

Kabaddi

A wonderful fast-paced team tag game from India.

How to facilitate the game

1 **Show the court.** The game takes place on a simple court, which is a rectangle on the ground with a half-way line.

2 **Demonstrate the game.**

- Each team of four or five children has one half of the court as their area. Teams take it in turns to attack.

- An attack consists of one of the team going over the half-way line and into enemy territory.

- When someone attacks, they have a bib tucked into their pocket or waistband (to make a tail). The attacker needs to try to tag the opponents waiting for them in that half of the pitch.

- The attacker tags their opponents by touching them anywhere on their body, and once they tag someone, that player is out of the game for the remainder of that attack and must leave the pitch (they come straight back in as soon as the attack is over).

- The challenge for the attacker is to try to tag all their opponents without getting their tail pinched.

- Teams take it in turns to attack, with team members taking it in turns to have a go.

3 **Add scoring.** Once the children have had a go at the game, introduce the following scoring system:

- The attacker gets a point for every opponent they can tag, or every opponent they can chase out of their half of the pitch – but only if they can then make it back into their own half without having their tail pinched.

- If their tail is pinched, they score zero points for that attack (so sometimes it might be best just to tag one or two opponents and then get back to your half of the court).

- Scores are accumulated, and you could play first team to ten points, or play a certain number of attacks each, or play to a time limit.

Assessment for learning

This game provides an interesting experience of competing as an individual while representing a team. Some children might love this experience, while others may really dislike it. It is worth reflecting on these feelings and considering how we might cope with this variety of competition.

- How did it feel to attack on your own? Why did you feel like this?

- How might we adjust the game to make everyone feel more comfortable and positive? (We could have pairs of attackers working together rather than individually.)

Aim

To represent your team as an individual and explore performing in front of others.

Set-up

Grouping:
Teams of four or five.

Equipment needed:
One bib per team and spots or lines to denote court boundaries.

Space needed:
Three courts are needed for a class of 30. Each court will host two teams competing against each other. See the diagram on page xvii for how to set up the court.

Cross-curricular link

This game originated in India thousands of years ago. Talented competitors play parts of the game with just one intake of air, repeating the word 'Kabaddi' until their breath runs out.

The Sport Education model

Sport Education is a curriculum model aimed at providing meaningful, realistic, and educationally rich experiences of sport and competition.

Why?

● To provide children with authentic, realistic and meaningful experiences and interactions.

● To help children to understand how to play the game; to value rules and ethics; and to participate positively and engage in appropriate behaviour.

● To help teach and learn important team values like loyalty, commitment and perseverance.

What?

Sport Education is an approach to the curriculum rather than a way of designing a single lesson. The model is intended to take place over a series of lessons, comprising a unit of work, for example. The model is typically used for games-based activities.

During the unit or series of lessons, children are grouped into teams. This is intended to replicate the experience of being in a team for a season (which many children might experience if they join a football club for example). Within the Sport Education model, children develop a sense of belonging to a team and experience the highs, lows, challenges and opportunities that team sport provides.

Children have the opportunity to take on a variety of different roles, including being a player, captain, coach and referee. You could also include other roles, such as statistician, reporter or equipment manager.

As with team sport, there is usually an accumulating event that the children are progressing towards, like a final or mini tournament.

How?

To make this model work, the teacher needs to spend time preparing materials and schedules. Materials that might be useful include simple job descriptions for the different roles (e.g. referee, coach).

Children need to be shown the game and explore the roles within each team. Establish strong rules around play and behaviours.

For primary-aged children, teams should be small enough for each child to feel a sense of involvement and belonging, but large enough to cover the variety of roles you have chosen to include.

Team names should be decided by the children. A team kit, perhaps just clothes in a certain colour, should be chosen. Children should take on roles and share them around so everyone gets an experience of different roles. One of the roles might be to agree a schedule of competition. It could be a good idea to use a school noticeboard to keep track of scores and progress.

The model could be adopted for a series of sequential PE lessons, or it could take place within the wider school context, for example with games at lunchtime and team practice in PE lessons, working towards a grand final at sports day.

See Wimbledon Doubles (page 223) for an example of a Sport Education lesson.

More information

● Pill, S. (2008), 'A teachers' perceptions of the Sport Education model as an alternative for upper primary school physical education', *ACHPER Healthy Lifestyles Journal*, 55, (2), 23–29.

● Penney, D., Clarke, G., Quill, M. and Kinchin, G. (2005), *Sport Education in Physical Education: Research based practice*. Abingdon: Routledge.

Wimbledon doubles

A pairs tennis tournament for Key Stage 2 using the Sport Education model.

How to facilitate the game

1 Show the courts. If you have time in the lesson, the children can help you set up, but if not, this needs to happen before the lesson. You will need four small courts, each with a net. The boundaries of each court should be marked out but you do not need all the other lines of a proper tennis court.

2 Introduce the event. Tell the class that they are going to have a doubles tennis tournament. Half the class will play the tournament and half will organise and manage it. Then they will swap over. It may be a good idea to prepare the pairs in advance, so they are of approximately equal ability.

3 Introduce the organisers. Explain the roles of the umpire, ball person and reporter (see page 224).

4 Demonstrate the game. The game will be a simple version of tennis. Serves will be underarm from the end of the court. They can land anywhere in the opposing side of the court. Teams and players will take it in turns to serve. It may help for the scoring system to be really simple, for example, play for ten minutes and whoever has most points wins. However, if you have time, you could teach the tennis scoring system.

5 Set up. Four games of doubles will take place at once. Each court will also have an umpire, two ball people, and a reporter. The reporter can be called on at any time by the teacher to give a brief report on the action. Scores should be recorded and a schedule devised so that everyone plays each other, or pairs progress towards a final.

6 Swap over. Ensure all children have an approximately equal time playing and organising.

Assessment for learning

The Sport Education model is intended to span several weeks, to lengthen the experience of playing, umpiring or reporting. Tennis equipment could be provided at playtime and lunchtime so children can practise. Reporters could report back to the school at assembly.

The below questions are intended to reflect on how we report on sport and competition. Typically, reporting will focus on the final score-line, but we may also need to think about how we tell the story of the game and what else is important beyond the result.

- What makes an interesting or engaging sports contest or competition?
- What makes a good sports report?
- What makes a good sports reporter?

Aim

To consider how we tell stories about sport and what we value in competitive contests.

Set-up

Grouping:
Whole class together.

Equipment needed:
Four courts marked out with spots or lines and a net across each court (this could be a length of rope or string); tennis balls and 16 tennis rackets.

Space needed:
The four courts can be small.

Eight children per court: four tennis players, an umpire, a reporter and two ball people.